Indian Poetry in English
A Comprehensive Study

Indian Poetry in English

A Comprehensive Study

Edited by

Vijay Kumar Roy

ADHYAYAN

ADHYAYAN PUBLISHERS & DISTRIBUTORS

New Delhi-110002

Published by
ADHYAYAN PUBLISHERS & DISTRIBUTORS
4378/4B, 105, J.M.D. House, Murari Lal Street
Ansari Road Darya Ganj, New Delhi - 110002
Ph.: 011-23263018, 011-23277156, Fax: 23280028
Email: adhyayanpublishers@yahoo.com

Indian Poetry in English
A Comprehensive Study

Edition 2011
ISBN 978-81-8435-277-1

Printed in India

Published by Harish Chandra Yadav for Adhyayan Publishers & Distributors, Delhi. Laser Typesetting at Jain Computers and Printed at Tarun Offset Printers, Delhi

Preface

The present book, *Indian Poetry in English: A Comprehensive study* is an addition to the increasingly growing interest in the realm of Indian English poetry both in India as well as in foreign universities. The book contains fourteen critical papers on well-known Indian English poets. It deals with the poetry of Henry Derozio, Toru Dutt, Sri Aurobindo, Rabindranath Tagore, Sarojini Naidu, AK Ramanujan, Keki N Daruwalla, Shiv K Kumar, Jayant Mahapatra, Niranjan Mohanty, Maha Nand Sharma, IK Sharma, Kamala Das, Mamata Kalia and Eunice De Souza.

Among all, Henry Louis Vivian Derozio (1809-31), the first Indian English poet, had a very brief literary career of about half a dozen years. His poetry is rich in Indian sensibility. Laxman Yadav has discussed Derozio's 'The Harp of India' which is one of his patriotic sonnets. He has discussed Derozio's patriotic feelings where the poet is proud of India's past glory and has love and respect for the great masters who produced divine music. But now time has changed, which causes grief to the poet.

Adwait Chaitanya has thrashed out the Indian ethos in the poetry of Toru Dutt (1856-77). He has described 'Sheaf' and 'Ancient Ballads and Legends of Hindustan' where there is abundance of Indianness. He has dealt with Dutt's use of characters like, Sita, Savitri, Lakshman, Uma, Dhruva, Prahlad and some others which confirm her great knowledge of Indian mythology even when she was a converted Christian.

Adwait Chaitanya's another paper is a detailed analysis of the mysticism in the poetry of Sri Aurobindo (1872-1950). He has explored Aurobindo's view that 'poetry is a sublime incantation' springing from the 'deep spiritual experience and self realization'. The paper deals with his major poems as 'The Bird of Fire', 'Trance', 'Shiva- the Inconscient Creator', 'The Life Heavens', 'Jivanamukta', 'Nirvana', 'Transformation', and 'Savitri' which reflect that Aurobindo's vision of poetry was imbued with mysticism.

The poetry of Tagore (1861-1941) has been discussed from several angles. Nirmal Sharma has dealt with "Spiritual consciousness in Gitanjali" and has elaborated Tagore's philosophy of 'manifestation of God', 'spiritual quest' and the influence of the Vedas and Upanishads. Another paper has brought out Tagore's real life experiences vindicated in his poetry that are generally overlooked. In this paper Amrita Tyagi has investigated romantic elements illustrating the lines of 'Kshanika', 'Unending Love', 'One Day in Spring', 'The Kiss', and 'The Gardener'. She has compared Tagore with Keats too.

Sarojini Naidu (1879-1949) has been discussed in depth and detail. Arti Kumari has investigated imagery in Naidu's poetry. She has described 'Palanquin Bearers', 'Nightfall in the City of Hyderabad', 'Golden Cassia', 'Vasant Panchami', 'Leilli', 'Life', 'Coromandal Fishers', 'Past and Future', 'Humayun to Zebeida', 'A Rajput Love Song', 'Dance of Love' and 'Gift of India' and has established the fact that the imagery and symbols make Sarojini Naidu a poet of high sensibility and imagination.

TR Joy's paper is quite focused and has highlighted the "Secular imagination" in poetry of AK Ramanujan (1929). He has dealt with 'Prayer to Lord Murugam', 'Salamanders' 'Death in Search of a Comfortable Metaphor', 'Daily Drivel: A Monologue', 'Figures of Disfigurement', and 'Children, Dreams, Theorems' and has examined Ramanujan's "secular way of creative engagement" .

Keki N Daruwalla (1937-), Shiv K Kumar (1921-) and Jayant Mahapatra (1928-) are prominent figures in Indian

English Literature. Jayshree Goswami, in a joint paper with Mojibur Rahman has described of Daruwalla's 'Caries' on the "discourse model" provided by Halliday. The paper deals with the "field", "tenor" and "mode" of the poem. It has a very intelligent analysis of the "prevailing corruption and loopholes in the political system" of India.

Jindagi Kumari in her joint paper with Rashmi Singh has discussed erotic aspect of Shiv K Kumar's poetry. They have highlighted vivid scenes of eroticism depicted in Kumar's poems such as 'Adam to God', 'The Face', 'To a Young Wife', 'Indian Women', 'An Indian Mango Vendor', 'A Young Female Jogger', 'Birth of Eve', 'Young Maidservant', 'To a Young Beautiful Woman Aspiring to be a Poet', 'Lolita', 'Voices at Night', and 'The Sea from a Cottage on the Beach'. The description of the ancient Indian erotic manuals *Kamasutra* of Vatsyayan, *Sringarasatak* of Bhartihari, *Gitagovinda* of Jaydev and *Padawali* of Vidyapati make the paper more significant.

Dinesh Panwar has discussed "Unvoiced Sorrow" and "pathetic conditions of women" depicted in poetry of Jayant Mahapatra (1928-). He has taken into account the women characters of the *Ramayana* and *Mahabharata* as well as the contemporary Indian women and has explored social discrimination, suffering and sacrifices continuing from the ancient times.

Ashok Kumar's paper is a detailed analysis of the poetry of Niranjan Mohanty (1953-2008). He has also brought into light Mohanty's teaching and literary career. Mohanty's "Saguna stream of poetry" has got main emphasis.

Indian women poets have significant place in Indian poetry in English. Bhavesh Chandra Pandey has dealt with the poetry of contemporary Indian women poets, like-Kamala Das, Gauri Deshpande, Mamata Kalia, Eunice D'Souza, and Lakshami Kannan. He has historically discussed the gender sensibility and the consequences of the fall of matriarchal system and the rise of patriarchal system in depth and detail.

RK Singh and Ram Kulesh Thakur's joint paper on "'Humour' as a Tool of Poetic Communication: A Comparative Study of Maha Nand Sharma and I.K. Sharma" is an excellent study of humour in the poetry of both the poets. The contributors have traced the history of humour and have gone through Aristotle, Plato, Immanuel Kant, Kierkegaard, Thomas Hobbes, Sigmund Freud, and Herbert Spencer and have come to the poetry of Maha Nand Sharma and I.K. Sharma. They have dealt with the "Rasa theory" in which 'hasya rasa' plays significant role in arousing humour in the reader.

Their second paper is a detailed analysis of sarcasm in poetry of Maha Nand Sharma and I.K. Sharma. They have examined that while the former creates sarcasm by introducing contrasting examples; the latter creates it through the use of language in a certain mode. The paper deals with the themes of discontentment and resurgence in the society as reflected in the poetry of both the poets.

I am grateful to the scholars who contributed their learned papers to this volume. I record my deep sense of reverence for Dr Subodh Kumar Sinha, Reader (Retired.) Department on English, L. N. Mithila University, Darbhanga for his kind support and encouragement in this work. I also record my sense of appreciation for Mr. Harish Chandra Yadav, Publisher of Adhyayan Publishers & Distributors, New Delhi for producing the book in this decent form.

—Vijay Kumar Roy

List of Contributors

1. **R. K. Singh,** Professor and Head, Department of Humanities and Social Sciences, Indian School of Mines, Dhanbad, Jharkhand.
2. **Mojibur Rahman,** Associate Professor, Department of Humanities and Social Sciences, Indian School of Mines, Dhanbad, Jharkhand.
3. **Bhavesh Chandra Pandey,** Senior Lecturer in English, S. K. R. College, Barbigha (Sheikhpura), T. M. Bhagalpur University, Bhagalpur, Bihar.
4. **T. R. Joy,** Lecturer, Department of English, Loyola College (Autonomous) Chennai, Tamilnadu.
5. **Ashok Kumar,** Department of English Language, State Council of Educational Research & Training, Narendranagar, Tehri Garhwal, Uttarakhand.
6. **Rajni Singh,** Assistant Professor, Department of Humanities and Social Sciences, Indian School of Mines, Dhanbad, Jharkhand.
7. **Dinesh Panwar,** Assistant Professor of English, Ajay Kumar Garg Engineering College, Ghaziabad, U. P.
8. **Nirmal Sharma,** Assistant Professor of English, S R M. University, NCR Campus Modinagar, Ghaziabad, U. P.
9. **Ram Kulesh Thakur,** Department of Humanities and Social Sciences, Indian School of Mines, Dhanbad, Jharkhand.

10. **Jayshree Goswami,** Department of Humanities and Social Sciences, Indian School of Mines, Dhanbad, Jharkhand.
11. **Jindagi Kumari,** Department of Humanities and Social Sciences Indian School of Mines, Dhanbad, Jharkhand.
12. **Laxman Yadav,** Department of English, Patna University, Patna, Bihar.
13. **Adwait Chaitanya,** Department of English, T. M. Bhagalpur University, Bhagalpur, Bihar.
14. **Amrita Tyagi,** Department of English, Lucknow University, Lucknow, U. P.
15. **Arti Kumari,** Department of English, B. R. A. Bihar University, Muzaffarpur, Bihar.

Contents

1

'The Harp of India': An Account of Derozio's Patriotism

Laxman Yadav

Henry Louis Vivian Derozio is a well-known name in Indian poetry in English. He was young, romantic and the first Indian poet to write in English. Half Indian and half Portugese by birth, it is he who ushered in the 'Age of Pioneers'. Like Keats, whom he admired intensely, he too died young at the age of twenty-two. One can only guess what he might have developed into had it been granted to him to realize his potentiality. As it is, we have only a handful of short lyrics and one long poem the 'The Fakir of Jungheera' by him.

Overshadowed by the great Romantic poets, Derozio showed the influence of their work on his own. When we read him, the impression we have is that he is another romantic poet. Such is the force of his talent and so naturally does the romantic diction come to him that he seems to be an authentic romantic poet, not a pale imitator. This similarity of temperament has been pointed out by a critic when he compares Derozio with Keats. Drawing a parallel between the two, he points out two features that the two poets had in common. Derozio had the same passionate, eagerly responsive temperament as Keats had, and like Keats he had the same sympathetic tie with nature. This passionate response to external events as well as to abstract ideas is seen, for example, in the sonnet entitled 'Poetry'.

> .... when the youthful brain is seized
> With that delicious frenzy which it loves,
> It raving reels, to very rapture pleased. (1-3)

In his attitude towards nature, Derozio is a follower of Wordsworth and like him, he often adds moral message to a poem devoted to nature. R. M. Williams finds Wordsworth's influence to be a bad one because of this tendency to moralize an idea.

The sonnet form is a favourite one of Derozio and he has written thirty sonnets. 'To the pupils of Hindu College', 'The Poet's Grave' and 'To India-My Native Land' are some of his best sonnets. There is a series of five Sonnets—'To Night' dealing with different aspects of the night. He does not, however, follow the rhyme scheme of different sonnets in a very faithful manner, nor does he always divide his sonnets into octave or sestet in the Petrarchan manner, or keep to the Shakespearean pattern.

One of the major themes in Derozio's poetry is love. He has written both sonnets and lyrics on this theme. It is interesting to note that love is treated in two different ways. On the one hand we have the customary romantic attitude towards love, that it is an ennobling and elevating emotion. On the other hand, we have love portraying the disappointment and despair of the lover.

We have in Derozio a poet of great promise. He did not have the opportunity of shaking off the influence of the great English poets who were his predecessors. His 'The Harp of India' is a very moving account of his patriotic feelings and at the same time it portrays the ethos of nineteenth century Bengal and the impact of the Western education on the middle class.

'The Harp of India' results from the complex socio-economic and socio-cultural climate of nineteenth century's colonial Bengal. Derozio himself was influenced by the Socio-economic situation of. He was one of the potent catalytic forces to bring about subsequent massive socio-cultural changes that can be seen at this time.

There is no denying the fact that Britishers established their reign in Bengal at first when they touched upon Indian soil, and as a result of which Calcutta became the focus of British administration, trade and commerce for the entire eighteenth century. Gradually there develops an amicable interaction between Britishers and Bengali elite in which the latter corroborate with the former i.e. ruling British in trade and commerce.

Some of the Bengali elites became partners with the ruling Britishers, earned unlimited wealth and became socially advantaged and consciously superior section of the society. They were economically dependent on land-rents and some other means. Other than the rise of British-Bengali Commerce, the factors that contributed to the social, cultural, religious and intellectual changes and activities in nineteenth century Bengal were: British Orientalism, the Christian Missionary activities, and the introduction to English education. "Derozio is regarded as the first Indian to write poetry in English. He is also often regarded as 'one of the stalwarts of modernism in the history of our nation." (Sengupta 1)

Even those critics and literary historians, who think Derozio had little poetic talent, have tried to cover up his 'poetic shortcomings' with his 'patriotic zeal'. M. K. Naik remarks that:

> A noteworthy feature of Derozio's poetry is its burning nationalistic zeal. ... Poems like 'To India-My Native Land',' The Harp of India' and 'To the Pupils of the Hindoo College' have an unmistakable authenticity of patriotic utterance which stamps Derozio as an Indian English poet who is truly a son of the soil. (23)

Naik goes on to say that though Derozio was a 'poet of slender actual achievement,' yet his poetry is redeemed by its 'patriotic zeal'. K. R. Srinivasa Iyengar has called Derozio "the first of our 'inheritors of unfulfilled renown," (34) and remarked that "Poor though his abilities may be, he will to his dying breath sing in defence and in praise of his country." (36)

Naik and Iyengar represent the standard response to Derozio. In the last ten years or so, there has been a major shift in perspective towards him. This shift is no doubt the result of our postmodern-postcolonial sensibility that does not anymore look at a text in the hitherto traditional way, but sees texts as socio-cultural codes and socio-historical documents and revisits, remembers and interrogates the texts of the colonial past for their discursive value.

The recent inclusion of Derozio in the undergraduate syllabus of Indian Universities is a part of the attempt to reclaim and canonize him, and to situate him at the beginnings of Indian nationalistic literature in English. Postcolonial critics such as Rosinka Chaudhuri situate Derozio among the first breed of the modern poets in colonial India to 'forge the language of nationhood' and to play a significant role in some of the earliest attempts at the 'creation and definition' of a modern Indian identity.

'The Harp of India' is one such poem of Derozio which displays his vision of the Indian nation and his pledge of allegiance to it. The construct of the poem is built around the central metaphor of the harp, a stringed, western musical instrument. Though the harp is anything but an Indian instrument, yet it would be wrong to doubt the poet's "Indianness" because of this seeming embezzlement. In fact, the curious selection of the harp as a metaphor of the then Indian situation is but emblematic of the east-west cultural interface in nineteenth century Bengal and the consequent mutation of sensibilities. More than anything, 'The Harp of India' symbolizes the ethos of nineteenth century Bengal and the impact of the Western education on the middle class at that time.

In 'The Harp of India', Derozio begins with an image that he might have got from Thomas Moore, reminiscent of conventional imagery in the late eighteenth century Celtic Revival in English literature. The natural strength as well as the limitations of the harp had provided an emblem of inspiration to the Romantic poets, and Derozio might also have had in mind Coleridge's *The Eolian Harp*, published in 1796. Yet the harp of Coleridge's poem was a redemptive Romantic symbol, while here, the symbol signifies a political enunciation of national deprivation. It is not that the harp of Derozio's poem is symbolic solely of 'national deprivation.' Though the poem begins on a note of dejection but at the end of the poem, the poet chooses to use the harp to trigger the country's regeneration. The harp that was 'Neglected, mute, and desolate' is thus transformed into an instrument of redemption.

The poem begins with a series of questions:

> Why hang'st thou lonely on you withered bough?
> Unstrung forever, must thou there remain;
> Thy music once was sweet-who hears it now?
> Why doth the breeze sigh over thee in vain?
> (1-4)

The poet sounds quite dejected and disheartened and seems to be rather pessimistic at the outset. The image of the 'withered bough' augments the atmosphere of desolation and dejection. The poet does not seem confident about his country's prospects. However, he fondly looks back to the past-"Thy music once was sweet." (3) The metaphor of the harp is expanded in these lines as the poet talks of the once sweet music of the harp which has no audience now. The effort of the breeze is thus wasted. The use of the word 'sigh' indicates that even the breeze is sad at the condition of the harp. The looking-back to the past glories shows the impact of British Orientalism on the poet: fervently asserting the former glories of the country while lamenting its current state of humiliation.

The second stanza begins thus:

> Silence hath bound thee with her fatal chain;
> Neglected, mute, and desolate art thou,
> Like ruined monument on desert plain: (5-7)

'Silence' is personified as a cruel master binding the harp with its deadly chains. The use of adjectives like 'mute', 'neglected', 'desolate' and 'ruined' further illustrates the intensity of the harp's misery. The image of the 'ruined monument' suggests that 'Life' seems to have abandoned the harp as it lies forsaken on an expanse of desert. The image of the 'ruined monument' in the desert is reminiscent of the closing words of Shelley's sonnet, 'Ozymandias' (1818) "boundless and bare/The lone and level sands stretch far away" and also of Shakespeare's sonnet No. 73: "Bare ruined choirs, where late the sweet birds sang."

The next few lines once again look nostalgically to the days of past glory:

> O! Many a hand more worthy far than mine
> Once thy harmonious chords to sweetness gave,
> And many a wreath for them did Fame entwine
> Of flowers still blooming on the minstrel's grave:
> (8-11)

Fame is personified as having 'entwined' wreaths of glory for the minstrels who churned out harmonious music from the harp. Derozio's cognizance of his gifted precursors shows that he must have read the Sanskrit poets in English translations by William Jones and his contemporary Orientalists. These flowers of glory, the poet says, are still in blossom. The poem ends on a positive note:

> Those hands are cold-but if thy notes divine

May be by mortal wakened once again,
Harp of my country, let me strike the strain!
(12-14)

The poet wants to begin an action of change; he no longer wishes the harp to remain merely as a remnant of the past hung on a 'withered bough'. He wants to bring the harp back to life. There is earnestness in the last line of the poem which indicates that the poet will, in reality, attempt to revive his country's lost glory. In the context of Derozio's life, these lines may be interpreted as the poet's efforts to awaken the people of his country to think rationally and to hear again the refrain of reason and change. The nationalist theme as well as Orientalist implication of the poem links it to Derozio's other famous sonnet, 'To India-My Native Land':

My country! In thy day of glory past
A beauteous halo circled round thy brow,
And worshipped as a deity thou wast.
Where is that glory, where that reverence now?
Thy eagle pinion is chained down at last,
And groveling in the lowly dust art thou: (1-6)

In both these sonnets Derozio was essentially making the same claim that he is an Indian and India is his native land, and that he wants to reclaim the lost honour and the past glory of his native land. If we situate these poems in the larger context of Derozio's poetry and his journalistic writings, an essential paradox comes to the fore; while in these sonnets he identifies himself as an Indian; in his journalistic writings he often identifies himself with the Europeans.

Reading 'The Harp of India' is thus problematized by issues of Derozio's multiple identity as a poet, teacher, journalist and Bengali/Indian/Eurasian. To form an idea of the complexities of Derozian thought one has to read him in totality: as a poet and as a journalist. Only then we may be able to get a holistic picture of this enigmatic personality.

Works Cited

Sengupta, Pallab. *Makers of Indian Literature,Derozio*. New Delhi: Sahitya Akademy, 2000.

Iyengar, K.R. Srinivasa. *Indian Writing in English*. New Delhi: Sterling, 2010.

Naik, M. K. *A History of Indian English Literature*. New Delhi: Sahitya Akademy, 2006.

Datta, Ketaki. *Indo-Anglian Literature: Past to Present*. Kolkata: Bookway, 2008.

Chattopadhyay, Goutam. *Bengal: Early Nineteenth Century-Selected documents*. Calcutta: Research Indian Publications, 1978.

2

The Unique Indianness of Toru Dutt

Adwait Chaitanya

Toru Dutt's poetry is uniquely Indian. Unique in the sense, that she was a Christian girl. Her father embraced Christianity only a few years after Toru's birth. So Toru was brought up in Christianity. This singles her out. Even Michael Madhusudan is not a pure exception, embracing Christianity later in life - from the rest of the Indo- Anglian poets who were all of them, unlike her, Hindus.

Toru Dutt was nurtured in Christianity in a unique way too. She was, so to say, no less a French than a British. She was as superb in English as she was in French. The fact is that her first major poetic work *A sheaf Gleaned in French Fields* is a rendering into English of a number of French poems. Her knowledge of both French and English was, to use the word of Margaret Macneil, "astonishing".

As a result of her rarely fast and rarely deep rooting in Christianity, she dug deep into English and French. And this gave birth to her French *Sheaf* rendered into English. It was no small achievement for any girl placed in her circumstances.

But far greater than this was her *Ancient Ballads and Legends of Hindustan*. This *Sheaf* Toru had gleaned from the Indian fields. This work brings her back to her real roots. It is remarkable that a girl who was steeped deep into Christianity and who died at around twenty should have chosen to study Sanskrit when she was about nineteen, and acquired a good knowledge of it within a few months. Indianness was thus in her very blood. It was her very soul.

In the *Ballads* Toru seems to have ultimately found her real self. B.N Talookdar writes:

> The most striking thing about the *Ancient Ballads* is that Toru is going back into her own nation after having been alienated from it for a long while by two foreign literatures. One year's work at Sanskrit and the inspiration of her earliest recollection of stories told by her mother bring her back to the very heart of India. Here all artificiality is banned, all superficiality has disappeared, only Toru remains, with roots which have just begun growing into her land. To ask how deep these roots would have grown is a matter of vain and melancholy speculation; it is enough to know that they are healthy and strong roots. (*Ancient Ballads and Legends of Hindustan* 30)

The *Ancient Ballads* is all Indian. It is, as a critic says, Toru Dutt's chief legacy to the posterity. It contains nine beautiful ballads: 'Savitri', 'Lakshman', 'Jogadhaya Uma', 'The Royal Ascetic and the Hind', 'Dhruva', 'Buttoo', 'Sindhu', 'Prahlad' and 'Sita', and miscellaneous poems. Toru's treatment of Indian myths is purely Indian. She does not anglicize her Indian themes. There is no romanticizing of these either. She recreates the ancient Indian ethos in her verses. She is completely Indian not only in the choice of her themes, but also in her outlook and treatment.

Toru does not romanticize her themes as, for example,

does Derozio. The latter romanticizes the theme of suttee. The theme is Indian. But Derozio's treatment of it is not so. Nor is Toru Dutt alienated from her own culture by staying abroad for a long period, as Manmohan Ghose is. She could never forget her great heritage. After her study of Sanskrit, her love for her father's legacy was deepened all the more. Though she had been brought up and trained in the western culture, she never forgot her roots, and she never ceased for a moment to be what she really was- an Indian.

The study of Sanskrit sharpened Toru's penchant for tasting the rich store of ancient Indian mythology, and gave it a new edge. The ancient legend of India was not alien for her, nor was the atmosphere thereof. These ancient themes stirred her heart and her imagination. The poems in the *Ballads* deal with individual episodes chosen from the Puranas and the great epics of India. Toru could hear the call of her ancestors and of her native land.

The nature of this call is truly oriental, nay, truly Indian. The culture of India is different from that of any other country on the globe. Some Indian critics who fail to understand the nature of their fathers' heritage give it the name of medievalism. Writing on the poetry of Toru Dutt, P.C Kotoky writes that Toru introduced "a kind of medievalism" (8) into Indo- Anglian verse. A. Dasgupta, on the other hand, finds the poetry of the *Ballads* perfect. The optimism of these poems is purely Indian. Dasgupta writes:

> This novelty in presentation and thought is the result of optimistic colour. This is Indian as well as modern, despite the fact that the poet revels in didacticism. What saves these poems from ethical prepossession is the poet's craftsmanship in the art of lyrical balladry marked with narrative simplicity. (11)

Toru Dutt is a true representative of Indian life and culture. Her ballads present poetic description of life in ancient India. She deals mythological Indian characters. She interprets mythology, culture, and philosophy. Through the medium of a foreign tongue, she successfully interprets the spirit of India to the West. She narrates the tales of ancient Hindu life and mythology with profound sympathy and enthusiasm. She presents the Hindu ideals of life and character with deep love and affection, and with force and vigour. She pours into her ballads her whole heart and her soul. Dr Kotoky writes: The poet's narratives are charged with lyric effusion of joy and pathos, anger and sorrow, anguish and hope, but these effusions do not disturb the easy flow of the narratives. (25)

The ballads of Toru have sublime themes and sublimity is the soul of Indian culture. These poems are in expression of Hindu thought and culture. It is beyond doubt that Toru's genius found its truest expression in Sanskrit literature. She found her inspiration in Indian culture. This was her good fortune. Had she taken inspiration from somewhere else, her poetry would not have been one and the same. Toru was an Indian, and a Hindu at heart. And the poems of the *Ancient Ballads* are the poetic embodiment of Hindu thoughts and culture.

Edmund Gosse, a great critic, is of the opinion that Toru's ballads breathe a Vedic solemnity and simplicity of temper. He finds them vitally devoid of littleness and frivolity. These ballads give us an insight into the very soul of India.

Toru is out and out an Indian. Sita's Hindu ideal of womanhood appeals to her most. She glorifies the ideal of Indian womanhood in 'Savitri', too. She glorifies the ideal of dignity of Savitri's character. Savitri, too, is an ideal wife like Sita. Worldly possessions are nothing to her. Like Maitreyi, she, too, attaches no value to worldly achievements. Toru describes in 'Savitri' the Upanishadic philosophy of the evanescence of this ephemeral world's temporal possessions. Though a Christian, Toru is a Hindu in spirit. Vedantic ideas find expression in her 'Savitri' and in her other poems. The doctrines of Karma and Maya have been highlighted by Toru in her ballads.

Sindhu is for Toru an ideal son who sacrifices his life for the sake of his parents. Buttoo is an ideal pupil who gives an ideal 'gurudakshina' to his guru. The pure and innocent Dhruva rises for, far above the highest of this earth. Lakshman is an ideal brother who sacrifices all his worldly comforts for the love of his brother. Prahlad vindicates the glory of god and the unflinching faith of the Lord's 'bhakt'.

Toru Dutt gave expression to her generous feelings towards the English and the French when she was a young girl. But even then she was a true Indian at heart. She was fully aware of the myths and legends of her dear native land and of her Great country's great culture. About the poetic melodies of Toru, Anant writes that they were "the melodies of Bengal, her native land, the melodies that she drank in so often that they now formed part of her very soul." (The Times of India, March 7, 1954)

Toru is the first Indo-Anglian poet who interpreted her culture to foreign lands and made the inhabitants thereof aware of the great Hindu ideas of which they could never have imagined. She was a converted Christian, but she had still a profound respect for Hindu gods and goddesses, heroes and heroines. This was so pleasantly rare of her. Her *Ballads* is steeped in Hindu tradition and Hindu ideals.

Works Cited

Macneil, M. *Poems by Indian Women.* Calcutta, London: OUP, 1921.

Jha, A.N. "Introductory Memoir", *Ancient Ballads and Legends of Hindustan.* (rpt.) Allahabad: Kitabistan, 1969.

Kotoky, P.C. *Indo-English Poetry.* Gauhati: Gauhati University Press, 1967.

Dasgupta, Alokranjan. "The Fragile Exotic Blossom of Songs", *Indian Literature,* vol. ix, No.2, 1966.

Anant. "Gifted Poetess", *The Times of India.* March 7, 1954.

Dunn, T.O.D. *The Bengali Writers of English Verse.* London, Bombay: Longman and Green Co. Ltd., 1918.

3

The Mysticism of Sri Aurobindo

Adwait Chaitanya

How ironic it is that he who was thought and planned to become a perfect westerner became the greatest revealer of the Vedas and the Upanishads of our modern times!

The poetry of Sri Aurobindo is a quest after the life divine. K. R. S. Iyengar writes that "...there was mystic fire and light in Sri Aurobindo's eyes, penetrating into the beyond; if Joan of Arc heard heavenly voices, Sri Aurobindo probably saw heavenly visions!" (151) Other poets too, might have seen such visions, but we cannot compare their mysticism with that of Sri Aurobindo. Other poets may be mystics and visionaries, but Sri Aurobindo is both a Yogi and a mystic. He is thus exceptionally rare as a mystic poet. His mysticism is no mere wordy exercise, but something felt in the blood.

The poetry of Sri Aurobindo is a type by itself. It is the poetry of the highest and rarest kind. It is the poetry of sublime incantation, of mystic vision, magical word and *mantric* vibration. It is a poetry that is born, as a critic opines, out of deep spiritual experience and self realization.

Sri Aurobindo's is an Upanishadic mysticism - higher than any other kind of mysticism. In his book, *The poetic Genius of Sri Aurobindo*, K. D. Sethna writes: "As a mystic poet, Sri Aurobindo's status is supreme and unique. Herbert has a religious simplicity at once piquant and passionate; Crashaw, a rich sensuousness kindling into spirituality; Donne, a nervous, intricate power troubling the Unknown; Vaughan, a half-obscure, half-bright straining beyond thought into mystical vision; Patmore, a pointed, polished ardour of the intellect for the veiled wonder; Francis Thomson, a restless and crowded and colourful heat of response to 'the many -splendoured Thing'. Wordsworth, Coleridge and Shelly are able only to flutter their wings in the sky of the Infinite, but they never reach Eternity; Yeats is too occult; Eliot too intellectual and pedantic and Blake too simple to reach the heights of Gnosticism. Other poets, including Tagore, are capable of dealing with one or two mystical planes, but Sri Aurobindo deals with all of them- occult, psychic and spiritual." (88-89)

Sri Aurobindo is the greatest mystic poet in the English language, not to be equalled in a thousand years. He is interested, unlike other poets, in the legend of the soul from where poetry, as he sees it, springs and where it finds its true enjoyer. To him, as Iyengar quotes, "The thinking of being is the fundamental manner of poeticizing...." (184) His poetry is in itself a class apart. It is a quest of the life divine. This poetry is mystic in all respects: for its visions, thoughts, themes, symbols, images, figures of speech and style. His poems and plays are, in the words of Iyengar, "an attempt to achieve in English verse something analogous to the Vedic *mantra.*" (166). Sri Aurobindo is of the "view that the 'future poetry'- even in English or especially in English - will more and more approximate to the *mantra.*" (166) This poetry comes from above:

> The voice of poetry comes from a region above us, a plane of being above and beyond our personal intelligence, a supermind which sees things in their innermost and largest truth by a Spiritual identity

> and with a lustrous effulgencey and rapture, and its native language is a revelation, inspired, intuitive word, limpid or subtly vibrant or densely packed with the glory of this ecstasy and lustre. *(The Future Poetry* 388)

Aurobindo's *Six Poems* are related to salvation. Even the poems of *Transformation and other poems* are like nature -mystic and spiritual. They are, in the words of Dwivedi, "Meditative, subtle and philosophical." (104) Of these six poems, 'The Bird of Fire' is a poem that is deeply mystic. The poet himself says about this poem: "The Bird of fire is the living vehicle of the gold fire of the Divine Light and the white fire of the Divine Tapas and the crimson fire of Divine Love - and everything else of the Divine Consciousness." Another poem of this group, 'Trance' reveals a higher plane of existence. The poet describes the state of the Yogi's mind that becomes, 'Vikalpa'-less. In other words, he describes that state of the mind whereby the Yogi experiences the 'Nirvikalpa Samadhi'. The mind sleeps to be simultaneously more wakeful:

> My mind is awake in stirless trance
> Hushed my heart, a burden of delight;
> Dispelled is the senses' flicker-dance,
> Mute the body aurate with light.
>
> (*Trance* 5-8)

When the mind is stirless, how can the senses flicker?

In 'Shiva- The Inconscient Creator', the poet depicts life as a self - rapt inconscient Force. The Poem, 'The life Heavens' summarizes one aspect of Sri Aurobindo's philosophy that true happiness and Eternal Reality can be attained only by maintaining a harmony between the physical and the Spiritual.

In his poems 'Jivanmukta' and 'Nirvana', Sri Aurobindo speaks of salvation and how to attain it. About the forms of these (i.e.'Jivanmukta'), he himself has observed: "The subject is the Vedantic ideal of the living man." Living, and at the same time, 'liberated'! What a seeming contradiction! This is the mysticism of the Indian master.

In his poem 'Transformation', the poet stands completely transformed, as all great mystics do, ready to receive the blessings of the Lord:

> I am no more a vassal of the flesh,
> A slave to Nature and her leaden rule;
> I am caught no more in the senses' narrow mesh.
> My soul unhorizoned widens to measureless sight,
> My body is God's happy living tool,
> My spirit a vast sum of deathless light. (9-14)

The same is the case with a large number of Sri Aurobindo's poem. His 'Last Poems' are also philosophical and mystic. The thought and the substance of all these poems are deeply spiritual and mystical.

Though the poem on which the fame of Sri Aurobindo chiefly rests is his 'Savitri'. It is a poem based on the legendary story of 'Savitri' and 'Satyavan' sung in seven cantos in the Vana Parva of the Mahabharata. This story has been narrated by Rishi Markandeya to Shri Yudhisthira. From this story we know of the power of wifely chastity and love.

Savitri is the daughter of Ashwapati, the king of Madra. Satyavan is the son of king Dyumatsena who has been dispossessed of his kingdom and lives in a hermitage. Savitri wants to marry Satyavan whom she has chosen to be her husband. She is told that Satyavan is to die after one year. She still persists in her choice in the face of this knowledge and is married to Satyavan. The Fateful day arrives. Satyavan dies and Yama takes his soul in his possession. Savitri follows Yama. The soul of Satyavan is tied to his noose. Savitri entreats the Lord of death to release her husband's soul. Asked by Yama to go back, she says that she must go wherever her husband was taken. There ensues a whole chain of arguments between

Yama and Savitri. Yama is pleased with her sweet and persuasive talk and asks her to demand a boon of him. She asks her boon so wisely that Yama gets trapped. He releases the soul of Satyavan, who comes back to life.

Sri Aurobindo imparts a cosmic significance to this simple story by the alchemy of his extraordinary genius. 'Savitri' is a mystic and transcendental poem told in spiritual symbols. It is a poem of the illumination of the Night Nescience by the transcendental light Divine.

All the important names in this poem have been used symbolically to describe the mystic states. Savitri herself embodies divine grace. In fact, the birth of Savitri has been possible by a boon from the Goddess Savitri. She is her incarnation- that is, the incarnation of Goddess Usha, the Mother of Eternal light, the World - Mother , who descended upon our agonized earth for the salvation of man. Savitri symbolises the light of Truth and Wisdom that struggles with darkness of Ignorance symbolized by the dark God, Yama, and overcomes it. Her struggle with the Lord of Death for the life of Satyavan is symbolic of the struggle of the human soul to break the blind chain of pre-determination.

This mystic poem begins with the description of the Dawn. The Dawn is symbolic of the light of creation and light of wisdom. And Night is here symbolic of chaos and Ignorance.

Ashwapati, the father of Savitri, is the symbol of life - energy or vital power. The very meaning of Ashwapati is the lord of life's energy. He symbolizes the soul of man that is in search of the Eternal Truth. For that he practises penance. But he feels that unless the Divine Mother incarnates herself down on earth, the world of Truth cannot be created. The Supreme Mother gives Ashwapati the boon that her own Grace would incarnate upon the earth. And thus, Savitri is born. Savitri- the Divine Grace, is the Divine Mother in the mortal frame of a worldly woman.

For divine perfection on this earth, the Divine Mother must have to be incarnated. Sri Aurobindo transforms the whole legend of the dispossessed Ashwapati's 'tapas' into an epic climb of the human soul in its journey from the inconscient to the very doorsteps of the Superconscient, and the whole symbol acquires a tremendous cosmic significance. The penance of Ashwapati symbolizes the trials and tribulations of the soul of Humanity for the attainment of truth. Man is a 'threshold' creature, and has thus a tremendous possibility in him of attaining perfect Divinity. Savitri is as much Divine as she is 'human'. Sri Aurobindo elevates the legend of Savitri and Satyavan to the highest plane of spirituality wherein cosmic purposes and intentions as well as human destiny have been brought into play.

Satyavan is nothing but the Truth, Eternal. And Truth is deathless. It cannot die. Satyavan rises from the domain of Death to the region of Eternity where the Sun of Truth never sets. He rises to the region where ignorance is unknown and death has no power. Savitri and Satyavan stay together in this region for some time and return thereafter to earth in order to accomplish their Divine work. This 'Work' is nothing else than the creation of a new Humanity. Savitri is thus the 'Sohar' (birth-song) of the new humanity -which Sri Aurobindo shows at the peak of this mysticism.

'Savitri' is a poem of Vedic symbolism and Upanishadic mysticism. The theme of this poem is eternity. In it we find man's fundamental problems of attaining immortality - that is, salvation. Reading through this poem is journeying through the mystic regions- the Gross, the Subtle, the Causal and the Transcendental. This poem is the poetic expression of Sri Aurobindo's divine, mystic vision. It is an experiment of mystic spiritual poetry cast into the symbolic mould.

Works Cited

Iyengar, K. R. S. *Indian Writing in English.* New Delhi: Sterling, 2010.

Sethna, K.D. *The Poetic Genius of Sri Aurobindo*. Bombay: Sri Aurobindo Circle, 1947.
Aurobindo, Sri. *The Future poetry*. Pondicherry: Sri Aurobindo Ashram, 1853.
Dwivedi, A. N. *Four Indo-Anglian Poets*. Bareilly: Prakash, 1981.
Aurobindo, Sri. *Six Poems*. Chandernagore: Rameshwar and Co., 1934.

4

Spiritual Consciousness in Tagore's *Gitanjali*

Nirmal Sharma

Spirituality is a journey from the outer world of names and forms to the subtle world of energies, to the innermost core of our being, the self. It can refer to an ultimate reality or transcendental dimension of the world; an inner path enabling a person to discover the essence of his or her being, or the "deepest values and meanings by which people live." Spiritual practices, including meditation, prayer and contemplation, are intended to develop an individual's inner life; such practices often lead to an experience of connectedness with a larger reality: a more comprehensive self; nature or the cosmos; and the divine realm.

Spirituality is often experienced as a source of inspiration or orientation in life. It can encompass belief in immaterial realities and experiences of the immanent or transcendent nature of the world. By consciousness we mean our level of perception about ourselves and the world around us, the higher the perception, the greater the consciousness. Those who have had the spiritual experience have noted that their state of awareness, i.e. their consciousness, has been elevated beyond the norm, enabling that person to experience existence from a whole new perspective. One of the most common experiences of this spiritual consciousness is feeling of "oneness." Oneness is often experienced as a feeling that everything is part of a whole, or that we all come from one common source and share a common spirit. To our ordinary perceptions, the world is a mass of individual life forms, each seeking its own destiny. Behind this appearance is the essential nature of existence, the One, Divine consciousness. This consciousness expresses itself in the universe in many forms, each with its own will to be. But in fact each form is an expression of the One seeking its infinite joy of existence. All true spiritual realization begins with this new perception of the essential Oneness of all beings and things.

Rabindranath Tagore, a multifaceted genius, a darling of versatility, was the most respected name in the literary-cultural world during his lifetime, in both the East and the West. He was not only the first Asian to receive the Nobel Prize for Literature (in 1913) but also only the second writer in English to receive it. Fondly dubbed 'Gurudev' by Mahatma Gandhi and 'eagle-sized lark' by Romain Rolland, his exquisite poetic power and gifted musical sensibility made him the author of the national anthems of three countries - India, Bangladesh and Sri Lanka - a feat still unmatched in history. He was knighted by King George V of England in 1915 and awarded an honorary doctorate by Oxford University in 1940.

He brought out the essence of Eastern spirituality in his poetry. His spiritual vision, as he himself said, is imbued "with the ancient spirit of India as revealed in our sacred texts and manifested in the life of today." (Sadhana vii) Swami Adiswarananda, Minister and Spiritual Leader of the Ramakrishna-Vivekananda Centre of New York in his Preface to "Tagore: The Mystic Poet" writes:

> Rabindranath Tagore's philosophical and spiritual thoughts transcend all limits of language, culture,

> and nationality. In his writings, the poet and mystic takes us on a spiritual quest and gives us a glimpse of the infinite in the midst of the finite, unity at the heart of all diversity, and the Divine in all beings and things of the universe. (www.americanpoems.com)

Tagore believed that "True knowledge is that which perceives the unity of all things in God." Through his vast body of immortal literary works, he taught us that the universe is a manifestation of God, and that there is no unbridgeable gulf between our world and God's. He was a spiritual man and had imbibed the ancient wisdom of India. He developed his philosophy of life through his personal experiences. He had all integral picture of God in his mind. He says that the self must have complete freedom. Freedom is needed even for union of self with God. Tagore accepts worldly values and says that one should not reject pleasure but it can never be the ideal of man. It has to be regulated by the spiritual nature of man. He synthesized individualism and universalism. His approach to philosophy was synthetic. Dr. K. D. Seth observes that:

> Rabindranath Tagore approached philosophy with a synthetic vision. The key to Tagore's position lies in this mediating quality as is manifest in his reconciling the extremes of transcendence and imminence, humanism and prapatti, naturalism and spiritualism, individualism and universalism in social life, freedom and determinism in human affairs, hedonistic aesthetic and activistic ethics, romanticism and realism, and beauty and ugliness in aesthetics. (145)

Tagore's *Gitanjali* or *Song Offerings* that contains his own English prose translation of Bengali poetry was published in 1913 with an introduction by the Irish poet W. B. Yeats. This book won Tagore the Nobel Prize for

Literature that year. Gitanjali is primarily a collection of 103 devotional songs translated by Tagore from his various poetical works in Bengali. It has been written in lyric tradition of Vaishnava Hinduism. The influence of study of Upanishads which he undertook accompanying his father Maharshi Debendranath Tagore, is clearly seen in the spiritual contours of the songs. The relationship between God and Man is the apparent core of all songs. Here this relationship has been looked at from different angles and herein lies the beauty of these songs. In his songs Tagore tries to find inner calm, a bliss that comes only with the experience of divine, and explores the themes of divine and human love:

> When one knows thee, then alien there is none,
>
> then no door is shut. Oh, grant me my prayer that
> I may never lose the bliss of the touch of the one
> in the
> play of the many.

(*Gitanjali,* LXIII)

Gitanjali thrives on Hindu mysticism and presents complex of thoughts. Tagore tries to establish an inseparable link between individual soul and greater soul. His mediations on God, man and nature, in the *Gitanjali,* not only echo the Vedantic awareness of the Absolute but also transmit the fervor of a *Vaishnava bhakta's* love for God. K R Srinivasa Iyengar points out that:

> The *Gitanjali* songs are mainly poems of *bhakti* in the great Indian tradition .... The current coin of India's devotional poetry is melted and minted anew by Rabindranath, but the pure gold shines as brightly as ever, even though the inscription on the coin is in English. The imagery, the conceits, the basic experience, the longing, the trial, the promise, and the realization –all have the quaintly unique Indian flavour and taste. (110-111)

Gitanjali represents the journey from finite to infinite. The songs in *Gitanjali* embrace the whole gamut of tender human feelings - love, humility, detachment, devotion, affection, dejection, and gratitude. W. B. Yeats believed that "A whole people, a whole civilization, immeasurably strange to us, seems to have been taken up into this imagination; ..." (Introduction 12)

Tagore's spirituality has humanitarian outlook. According to him God is not in temple and in other outward worldly things. He lives in the heart of those people who are simple, hard working and without pretension:

> Whom dost thou worship in this lonely dark corner of a temple with doors all shut? Open thine eyes and see thy God is not before thee!
> He is there where the tiller is tilling the hard ground and where the path maker is breaking stones. He is with them in sun and in shower, and his garment is covered with dust.
>
> (XI)

This journey to infinite begins with imagining God as flute player and poet himself as flute:

> Thou hast made me endless, such is thy pleasure. This frail vessel thou emptiest again and again, and fillest it ever with fresh life.
>
> (I)

Boundless admiration for Master's skill in music overwhelms the disciple:

> I know not how thou singest, my master! I ever listen in silent amazement.
> The light of thy music illumines the world. The life breath of thy music runs from sky to sky. The

> holy stream of thy music breaks through all stony obstacles and rushes on.
>
> (III)

Humility for Tagore is the mean of communion with the Master who sits on the throne:

> Here is thy footstool and there rest thy feet where live the poorest, and lowliest, and lost.
>
> (X)

Gitanjali has poems of detachment and the earthly defenses crumble in them. This is apparent in the following lines:

> I know that the day will come when my sight of this earth shall be lost, and life will take its leave in silence, drawing the last curtain over my eyes.
>
> (XCII)

The poet gives considerable thought to the stern reality of death, but death is not painted as dark, grey or fearsome, instead death is powered by the poetic touches of Tagore:

> On the seashore of endless worlds children meet. .... Tempest roams in the pathless sky, ships get wrecked in the trackless water, death is abroad and children play. On the seashore of endless worlds is the great meeting of children.
>
> (LX)

Tagore believes in the concept that soul on earth pines for the union with God. Here it is only for short time. So for this union, poet wants to welcome death. It is only through death that the soul can leave the body and can attain God,

> O Thou, the last fulfillment of life, Death, my death, come and whisper to me!
>
> (XCI)

He knows the importance of death so he offers his guest (death) "the full vessel of my life- I will never let him go with empty hands." (XC) The poet is very happy for the unification of his soul with God. The journey to infinite ends with complete surrender and thereby merges with infinite spirit. The poet is a great devout and takes every possible effort to mingle with the Almighty:

> The flowers have been woven and the garland is ready for the bridegroom. After the wedding the bride shall leave her home and meet her lord alone in
> the solitude of night.
>
> (XCI)

Again he says:

> In one salutation to thee, my God, let all my senses spread out and touch this world at thy feet.
>
> (CIII)

Tagore has maintained the unity by coalescence of the themes. *Gitanjali* is indigenous in its content. K. R. Srinivasa Iyengar truly calls it "poetry unmistakable". It is a kind of spiritual therapy for the ailing souls. Yeats's observation is also similar; he sees its long lasting relevance: "...as the generations pass, travellers will hum them on the highway and men rowing upon rivers. Lovers, while they await one another, shall find, in murmuring them, this love of God a magic gulf wherein their own more bitter passion may bathe and renew its youth." (Introduction 11)

Tagore was a solitary pilgrim whose quest was nothing but ceaseless bliss, which is beyond mundane experience. He devoted his life in search of transnational and universal form of religious and spiritual expression, rooted at the same time in Indian ethos. He writes:

> This is my prayer to thee, my lord—strike, strike at the root of penury in my heart. ...
> Give me the strength to raise my mind high above daily trifles.
> And give me the strength to surrender my strength to thy will with love.
>
> (XXXVI)

Tagore wrote and spoke about the divinity of nature; a 'super-soul' permeated all things. He wrote of the 'humanity of God' and of the 'divinity of man'. All 'true knowledge and service' emanate from the One. 'Service,' he famously said, is 'joy'. Haroild Hjärne, presenting Tagore the Nobel Prize, said:

> He peruses his Vedic hymns, his Upanishads, and indeed the theses of Buddha himself, in such a manner that he discovers in them, what is for him an irrefutable truth. If he seeks the divinity in nature, he finds there a living personality with the features of omnipotence .... Ascetic and even ethic austerity would appear to be alien to his type of divinity worship, which may be characterized as a species of aesthetic theism. Piety of that description is in full concord with the whole of his poetry, and it has bestowed peace upon him. He proclaims the coming of that peace for weary and careworn souls even within the bounds of Christendom. (http: nobel prize.org)

The music of the songs too is his own. Through it, in a way, traditional to his culture but with a spirit unique to him, he expresses his love for God and man, his vision of the beauties of nature and the human heart, and his pride in his native land. The images he uses are sometimes the old religious ones of the love between man and woman, as representative of the love between man and God; and sometimes they are drawn from the complex life of Kolkata. His portrayal of the relationship between life and death is very lively:

> The child cries out when from the right breast the mother takes it away, in the very next moment to find in the left one its consolation.
>
> (XCV)

Thus the poems of *Gitanjali* express a largely metaphysical outlook, taking about a union with the 'supreme'. There is in it a mystic intoxication which gives supernal ecstasy and joy. It puts in a nutshell the experience of delight of being with the divine- which surpasses everything. W. B. Yeats asserts in his memorable 'Introduction' to *Gitanjali*: "I read Rabindranath every day, to read one line of his is to forget all the troubles of the world."(5)

Undoubtedly, "The one hundred odd songs in *Gitanjali* form a mighty piece of prayer and pleading and exultation." (Iyenger 112) "M. Abbe Bremond once declared that pure poetry aspires to a condition of prayer. Such poetry is half a prayer from below, half a whisper from above: the prayer evoking the response, or the whisper provoking the prayer, and always prayer and whisper chiming into song. Gitanjali is full of such poetry." (Quoted by Iyenger 111)

Here poet has synthetic spiritual vision. He talks from physical to metaphysical, materialistic to spirituality and finite to infinite. Through the poems of *Gitanjali,* the poet tries to attain the highest reality that is God. As he confesses in the second last poem: "I boasted among men that I had known you. They see your pictures in all works of mine."(CII) According to him, not only in *Gitanjali* but in all his works, he has spiritual consciousness: "From the words of the poet men take what meanings please them; yet their last meaning points to thee." (LXXV)

Works Cited:

Tagore, Rabindranath. *Gitanjali*. (Introduction by W. B. Yeats) New Delhi: Macmillian, 2000.

Das, Subhamoy. *The Mysticism of Rabindranath Tagore*. About.com:Hinduism.

Tagore, Rabindranath. *Tagore: The Mystic Poets* (preface by Swami Adiswarananda). Woodstock, Vermont: Skylight Paths Publishing, 2004.

www.americanpoems.comstwww.americanpoems.com

Pandey, R. S., ed. *Educational Thoughts*. New Delhi: Adhyayan Publishers, 2006.

Iyengar, K. R. Srinivasa. *Indian Writing in English*. New Delhi: Sterling, 2010.

Frenz, Horst. "The Nobel Prize in Literature 1913", *Nobel Lectures, Literature 1901-1967*. ed. Amsterdam: Elsevier publishing Company, 1969. Nobelprize.org.

http:nobel prize.org/Nobel-prize literature/laureates/ 1913/

5

Genuine Human Feelings and Emotions in the Poetry of Tagore

Amrita Tyagi

Tagore's reputation as a 'Maharshi' and 'Gurudev' has created a kind of veil through which neither we can see a normal human being nor appreciate his genuine emotions and sensibilities. Under the influence of the greatness and supremacy of his personality, we find ourselves unable to identify the direct influence of human experience even in his normal dealings of life. Height of his greatness always drags us from penetrating into this veil and finding out the real feelings and emotions which lay buried in his poetry. "Ajitkumar Chakravarti, Srikumar Banerjee, Mohitlal Majumdar, or Charuchandra Banerjee either refused to consider the direct influence of the human experiences, especially his relationships with various women, on some of Rabindranath's greatest lyrical pieces, or considered any attempt to probe into them irrelevant, irreverent, or irresponsible." (Sil) It seems that they always study Tagore having his spell-bound personality in their minds, and their mindsets do not let them to look for real Tagore, as a human being, in the fog of his images, they have.

There are common passions, emotions and sensibilities of a normal person in Tagore's life, especially in his dealing with love. For looking a real Tagore in-between, we have to have some pieces of his life and the glimpses of the atmosphere in which he was brought up. The circumstances and the growth of Tagore were uncommon; moreover he lived a confined life in a highly disciplined and cultured family. Tagore's grandfather, Prince Dwarika Nath, was a friend of Ram Mohan Roy, his father Maharishi Devendra Nath was the power behind the 'Brahmo Samaj' in its palmy days, such were his antecedents. Affluent and aristocratic culture surrounded him. It was an atmosphere of expectancy and it shaped child Tagore into the frame which was formed by his background and circumstances. Though under the instruction of his father he lived a Spartan and measured life, but this is the recurring feature of his creative life. The passionate and sensitive feelings of an adolescent come out, his heart dances with peacocks dancing in the rain. The whirling movements lend itself easily to dance by a girl for whom Tagore supplies a lovely libretto. In *Kshanika* (1901), we can perceive the passionate heart of an adolescent:

> My heart dances today like a peacock, it dances, dances....
> New woodland grass...
> Who wanders high on the palace-tower, hair unravelled, unravelled
> Pulling her cloud-blue sari
> Close to her breast?

Emphasizing on spiritual and philosophical dimensions, we readily realize that he was truly another great poet of his days. Like other romantic poets, Tagore was a man of moods and with many masks, to touch the core will never be easy, it needs penetration into the depths of his poetry. Along with religious and patriotic Tagore there is sensuous, shy as well as passionate Tagore. In fact it is Tagore's delicate and refined sensibilities that dictated his poetic imagination. When we examine Tagore's own unbridled desire for women we find him a romantic young man with no sacred and sublime feelings. He himself confessed "I never been able to forget her (an attractive and emancipated Maharashtrian girl whom he met during his stay at Ahmedabad with his brother). Surprisingly it is a fact that he never forgot the lady. Memory lingered as 'Bhagna Hridya' (broken heart). But he was made to suppress his feelings as his father asked him to write some devotional songs for congratulatory chapel as a cure for his heartache or *vedena*. This romantic agony can be felt in "*sandhya sangeet*" (evening song). The heart's wilderness, as he called it, was so sad so sweet. "I have lost my ways". The young poet's heart was shivering in trepidation having been overcome by an uncontrollable longing for the mysterious body's touch. He writes:

> My ecstatic heart seeks you in daring desperation,
> Asking how could I get near you?
> How could I fill the void in my heart that you created?

We can witness here how he had to compel himself to divert his feelings from a girl to God.

A cold chronological account might miss the real issue, and would not be the best method for us here, what we propose to do is to procure few pearls-not all-and briefly point out my views. Mansi is nicely ambiguous: it means 'conceived by mind fancy' or 'sweet heart of one fancy'. It is also a common name for Bengali women. Tagore gave life and shape to his imagination of romantic and mysterious women in the portrayal of Mansi. The youthful poet stirred out by the tender emotions (Unending Love):

> In life after life, in age after age, forever. ...
> Whenever I hear old chronicles of love, it's age old pain,

> It's ancient tale of being apart or together.
> As I stare on and on into the past, in the end you emerge,
> Clad in the light of a pole-star, piercing the darkness of time.
> You become an image of what is remembered forever.

Like Romantic poets Tagore is a poet of hope. He is well aware of the suffering and distress in love. He writes in the same poem:

> At the heart of time, love of one for another.
> We have played alongside millions of lovers,
> Shared in the same shy sweetness of meeting,
> the distressful tears of farewell,
> Old love but in shapes that renew and renew forever.

His longing and waiting for an unknown beloved is obvious in the following lines of 'One Day in Spring':

> One day in spring, a woman came
> In my lonely woods,
> In the lovely form of the Beloved.

Like common lovers, he dreams of his beloved and hesitates before her. The imaginative quality of the poem reaches its climax when he writes that she

> Glanced at my face, made sad with pain,
> And with quick steps, came and sat by me.
> Taking my hands in hers, she said:
> 'You do not know me, nor I you—
> I wonder how this could be?'
> I said:
> 'We two shall build, a bridge for ever
> Between two beings, each to the other unknown,

The poet is an 'eager wonderer' and believes that 'The cry that is in my heart is also the cry of her heart;/The thread with which she binds me binds her too.' (One Day in Spring) The poem reflects the true experience of love. The poet vindicates such experience again in the following lines:

> Crossing the wide oceans, she came to steal my heart.
> She forgot to return, having lost her own.
> Her own charms play traitor to her,
> She spreads her net, knowing not
> Whether she will catch or be caught.

His romantic craving is more intensified in 'The Kiss':

> Lips' language to lips' ears.
> Two drinking each other's heart, it seems.
> Two roving loves who have left home,
> pilgrims to the confluence of lips.
> Two waves rise by the law of love

Unlike the early mood of his adolescence when he seeks the abstract and idealized women of his fancy, he, a fully grown up young man, constructs the image of a realistic female, displaying an erotic love, *prem*. He wishes to have that physical beauty, he creates in *Mansi*. Some glimpses of this kind of feelings can be perceived in *The Gardener*, next only to *Gitanjali*, the richest collection of love poetry with a human rather than a divine slant. These songs are expression of intense sensual desire. When Tagore breathes his lyre, vivid imagery full of passionate feelings breaks out into a sudden life like a spark:

> I run as a musk-deer runs in the shadow of the forest, mad with his own perfume.
> The night is the night of mid-May, the breeze is the breeze of the south.

> I lose my way and I wander, I seek what I cannot get, I get what I do not seek.

This poem is equally important in this context in which the poet clearly mentions his real feelings and emotions which make one poet. The poem is full of imagery and with the help of a bird the poet vindicates the intense feelings of a lover to meet his beloved where restrictions prevent them to meet each other:

> Their love is intense with longing, but they never can fly wing to wing.
> Through the bars of the cage they look, and vain is their wish to know each other.
> They flutter their wings in yearning, and sing, 'Come closer, my love!'
> The free bird cries, 'It cannot be, I fear the closed doors of the cage.'
> The cage bird whispers. 'Alas, my wings are powerless and dead.'

All these imaginings, make-believe and love-play make us believe that lover of Tagore had to face all agony and hopelessness, ecstasy and fulfillment which a normal person face in his course of life.

Above verses point out that the main characteristic of love poetry of Tagore are 'yearning and longing.' He is rather a poet of *virah* than *Milan*. The longing, yearning and even confusion of Tagore which is explicit in above lines can be discerned in Tagore's own confession to the husband of his niece Pramatha Choudhary, "I can't tell you for sure whether I'm driven by (human) love with all its pleasure and pains deriving from union and separation"

If we look at the entire output of his love poetry, we readily find Tagore, the poet, quite other than what he has been taken. There is a strong undercurrent of powerful feelings and emotions beneath all his images he uses, experiences and depicts; there are joys and sufferings, confusion and tensions that are the very conditions of genuine human feelings in the poetry of Tagore.

Works Cited:

Sil, Narasingha P. *Devotio Humana: Rabindranath's Love Poems Revisited.* www.prabaas.com

Majumdar, Mohit Lal. *Adhunik Bangla Sahitya.* 7th ed. Kolkota: General Publishers, 1973.

Banerjee, Sri Kumar. *Rabindra Srishti Samiksha.* Kolkata: Orient Book, 1946.

Ghosh, Sanka. *Kabir Abhypraya (The Poet Intentions).* Kolkata: Papyrus, 1998.

6

Imagery in the Poetry of Sarojini Naidu

Arti Kumari

Sarojini, 'The Nightingale of India', emerged on the literary scene at the time when sonnet with its discipline, ode with its call to higher thoughts and lyric with its emphasis on colour and imagery were in vogue. Although brought up in romantic tradition and fed solely on the ornate poetry of the East and West, she remains typically romantic in her taste and temperament, sensibility and art. She never tries poetry after the modern fashion nor does she approve of its lack of passion. For all her adoption of English as her medium of poetic expression, she remained rooted firmly to her soil. The themes, thoughts and even the imagery she employs in her poems are typically native in spirit and character. She captures the atmosphere and the heart of her native land with its flowers and birds, aspects and events, people and occupations. The images are delicate, sensuous and romantic, like "the dance of the dew on the wings of moonbeam".

Sarojini is a poet of keen sensibility and rich imagination, and her poetry offers a delightful feast of similes and metaphors. She expresses her feelings through sensuous imagery which is usually highly imaginative and suggestive. Not only her sense perceptions are quick and alert, she also has a rare gift of communicating these perceptions by vivid, picturesque and sensuous imagery. V. S. Narvane on her imagery, specially on its Indian character, writes:

> However the strongest feature of Sarojini's poetry is her vivid imagery. Her most memorable lines are those in which she has presented beautiful and graphic pictures by fusing together several visual impressions. It should be stressed, once again, that these images can be appreciated only by those who have retained their sensitivity to the subtle stimuli which come from the Indian environment, and who still have a feeling for aspects of Indian life now rarely experienced in our modern cities. (139)

'Palanquin Bearers' is a simple folk song, depicting a vanished aspect of rural life. The poem gains richness through the images which lie inherent in the native consciousness. The quick succession of images shows the Shelleyan impact. The noble lady inside the palanquin has been compared to a number of objects:

> Lightly, O Lightly, we bear her along,
> She sways like a flower in the wind of our song;
> She skims like a bird on the foam of a stream,
> She floats like a laugh from the lips of a dream,
> Gaily, O gaily we glide and we sing,
> We bear her along like a pearl on a string. (1-6)

There is a sumptuous feast of images for the reader's delight. The lady "sways like a flower", "skims like a bird", "floats like a laugh" and the palanquin bearers bear her along "like a pearl on a string". James Cousin does not find any thought in the poem but he is impressed by its imagery and romantic setting. He comments that the poem "is without the slightest suspicion of literature, yet its charm is instantaneous and complete". The images indicate a lightness of touch, buoyancy, and create a dreamlike atmosphere.

Sarojini is a tender child of nature who responds with a wide-eyed wonder and excitement to the sights, sounds and smells of nature. Nature lies before her spread out with beauties and wonders, and all her senses reach them with delight and excitement. Natural phenomena, animate or inanimate, stir her deeply and her response is at once direct and intense. Her quick response to the endless variety and countless colours of the world around her, results in a poetry that is at once gorgeous and ornate with a rich tapestry of images. Sarojini's pictorial power is tremendous. The artistic method she employs in her poems is that of picking out the theme in sharp outlines, and presenting the idea concretely through visual images and rich diction. In 'Nightfall in the city of Hyderabad', the images employed are precise and evocative. The splendour and beauty of the royal city is captured beautifully by the natural imagery:

> See how the speckled city burns like a pigeon's throat,
> Jewelled with embers of opal and peridote,
> See the White river that flashes and scintillates,
> Curved like a tusk from the mouth of the city-gates. (1-4)

The image of the star-studded sky burning like a pigeon's throat is picturesque and romantic. The sky at nightfall in the "city burns like a pigeon's throat; perhaps like a thought of a bride whose throat quivers wit glittering ornaments. Another evocative image appears in the concluding lines where night is imaged as the majestic arrival of a queen:

> Over the city bridge Night comes majestically,
> Borne like a queen to a sumptuous festival. (13-14)

In 'Golden Cassia', the string of metaphors pictures the flowers in their exotic splendour. The poet discovers that they are more than mere woodland flowers scattered on the way. They have been compared with various objects. They are "like some new -fallen star" or "the golden lamps for a fairy shrine" or "the golden pitchers for fairy wine" or "the glimmering ghosts of a bygone dream". But some very striking images appear in the following lines:

> Perchance you are, O frail and sweet!
> Bright anklet-bells from the wild spring's feet,
> Or the gleaming tears that some fair bride shed
> Remembering her lost maidenhead. (7-10)

The poet conceives of spring as a woman wearing anklet in her feet. The image of bright anklet bells from a maiden's feet is quite startling. The mixed feeling of joy and pain of the Indian bride is imaged suggestively in "the gleaming tears that some fair bride shed/ Remembering her lost maidenhead."

Sarojini Naidu skilfully blends memory with desire and projects a natural thing as an image of pure delight and profound beauty. In 'Vasant Panchami' the poet employs natural imagery to intensify the effect and enhance the thematic appeal. The poem has a native flavour, and it is written in the vein of Hindi poetry. The young widow's grief-stricken heart is like "sorrow-trodden grass". Her dark and dry life is like a "fallen flower and faded leaf":

> For my sad life is doomed to be, alas,
> Ruined and sere like sorrow-trodden grass,
> My heart hath grown, plucked by the wind of grief,
> Akin to fallen flower and faded leaf,
> Akin to every lone and withered thing
> The hath forgone the kisses of the spring. (25-30)

'Leilli' is a nature poem with a Muslim theme but Hindu ethos. In her best moments of inspiration, she writes this poem in which western romantic and Indian classical idioms interact with one another. In this poem, the poet blends English, Persian and Sanskrit conventions imaginatively to produce something that is highly suggestive and individual. 'Leilli' is a Persian word for night. The first stanza suggests the approach of night through concrete images. The natural imagery employed here beautifully sets the scene of night's quietude:

> The serpents are asleep among the poppies,
> The fireflies light the soundless panther's way
> To tangled paths where shy gazelles are straying,
> And parrot-plumes outshine the dying day,
> O soft! the lotus-buds upon the stream
> Are stirring like sweet maidens when they dream.
> (1-6)

The second stanza makes us feel the mighty presence of night. Night is personified and enshrined in the forest temple. The entire forest makes a temple where winds are seen dancing and swooning at the holy feet of night. The atmosphere created lends a sublime holiness to the night. The image of moon shining "as a caste-mark" on the brow of Heaven is a great achievement in itself:

> A cast-mark on the azure brows of Heaven,
> The golden moon burns sacred, solemn, bright
> The winds are dancing in the forest-temple,
> And swooning at the holy feet of Night,
> Hush! in the silence mystic voices sing
> And make the gods their intense-offering. (7-12)

James Cousins responds rapturously to this caste-mark image. He observes that,

> "The figuring of the moon as a caste-mark on the forehead of heaven is in itself a unique achievement of the imagination in poetry in the English

> language. It lifts India to the literary heavens: it threatens the throne of Diana (the goddess of Moon in the Roman mythology) of the classics; it releases Luna (another name for the goddess Moon) from the work of asylum keeper (Luna is also associated with lunacy: madness), and gives her instead the office of remembrances to Earth that the Divine is imprinted on the open face of Nature." (265)

The major part of her poetry has been composed in her youth. Hence it has always a glow with her vigorous imagination and youthful fancy. Her poetry is, naturally, marked by a freshness of imagination which transforms common objects of nature and human life into something miraculously fresh and uncommon. In 'Life' the poet employs vivid and concrete images to set the children's innocent world of colour and fantasy. In childhood, life is full of rosy dreams: it is like "a lovely stalactite". The image of life as 'a lovely stalactite' is highly suggestive of children's world of careless joy. There is a kinetic image also. The morning is suggested beautifully by the image of the sea billows leaping in the flames of amber and amethyst. It is morning time hence one can easily imagine a play of colours on the leaping waves. Both the images build up the children's world of joy and dreams:

> Life is a lovely stalactite of dreams,
> Or carnival of careless joys that leap
> About your hearts like billows on the deep
> In flames of amber and amethyst. (2-5)

Sarojini is a gifted artist who shows, all through the corpus of her poetry, a great flair for ornamental and highly sophisticated style which abounds in lovely similes, metaphors, images and symbols. Her imagery is highly influenced by Shelley, Keats, Masefield, early Yeats and Tagore who had a lot of romanticism in their world of imagery.

'Coromandal Fishers' is a perfectly realized lyric which depicts the happy, busy life of the fishers who go out with the morning light. It reflects the folk spirit and subtle atmospheric beauty of the sea. The sensuous and romantic imagery in the following lines is quite appealing:

> Sweet is the shade of the coconut glade, and
> the scent of the mango grove,
> And sweet are the sands at the full O'the
> moon with the sound of the voices we love.
> But sweeter, O brothers, the kiss of the spray and
> the dance of the wild foam's glee;
> Row, brothers, row to the blue of the verge,
> where the low sky mates with the sea. (9-12)

The impact of Wordsworth can be felt distinctly on the imagery. The image of "the dance of the wild foam's glee", is reminiscent of Wordsworth's golden daffodils: "The waves beside them danced, but they/Outdid the sparkling waves in glee". There is another startling image in "blue of the verge, where the low sky mates with the sea." Sea is a dream to the fishermen, a dream they must pursue afresh every day.

'Past and Future' has distinct echo of Tennyson on its imagery. It is a poem consisting of two stanzas, each offering a memorable image. In the first stanza the past has been visualized as a mountain cell where old hermit's memories dwell in consecrated calm:

> The new hath come and now the old retires:
> And so the past becomes a mountain-cell
> Where lone, apart, old hermit-memories dwell
> In consecrated calm, forgotten yet
> Of the keen heart that hastens to forget
> Old longings in fulfilling new desires (1-6)

These lines are reminiscent of Tennyson's lines in 'Morte D'Arthur':

> The old order changeth, yielding place to new
> And god fulfills Himself in many ways,
> Lest one good custom should corrupt the world.

Future is unknown and uncertain hence it is aptly imaged in the second stanza as a timid person:

> Like a strange, fated bride as yet unknown,
> His timid future shrinking there alone,
> Beneath her marriage-veil of mysteries. (11-13)

Sarojini's love poems are steeped thoroughly in romantic imagery. 'Humayun to Zebeida' offers a number of delicate images. Zubeida, the beloved haunts her lover's 'waking like a dream', his 'slumber like a moon', and 'pervading him like a musky scent' and possessing him like a tune. Humayun, the lover wishes to be possessed by his beloved. He expresses his feeling of love through a string of similes which throw up lovely images:

> You haunt my waking like a dream, my slumber like a moon,
> Pervade me like a musky scent, possess me like a tune. (3-4)

A string of metaphors distinguishes the poem 'A Rajput Love Song'. The dawn has separated the lovers to join again at night. The beloved, Parwati is not worried at all, for her love is constantly with her in the form of the 'basil wreath' in her 'tresses', the jewelled golden bangle on her hand, the scent of the 'keora' in her clothes, the 'vermilion tassel' in her 'girdles', 'the scented fan' on her 'pillow' and the 'sandal lute' or the' silver lamp' in her 'shrine'. She expresses her passionate longings of love through a chain of images, all drawn from a woman's delicate world:

> O Love! Were you a basil-wreath to twine among my tresses,
> A jewelled clasp of shining gold to bind around my sleeve,

O Love! Were you the keora's soul that haunts
my silken raiment,
A bright, vermillion tassel in the girdles that I
weave;
O Love! Were you the scented fan
that lies upon my pillow,
A sandal lute, or silver lamp that burns before my
shrine. (1-9)

'Dance of Love' speaks of the ecstasy and pain of love in the heart of the lovers. The sweet music and the subtle stepping of dance wake in their heart strange aches and ecstasies which have been appropriately supported by the sensuous imagery:

The music sighs and slumbers,
It stirs and weeps again...
Hush, it wakes and weeps and murmurs
Like a woman's heart in pain;
Now it laughs and calls and coaxes,
Like a lover in the night,
Now it pants with sudden longing,
Now it sobs with spent delight. (1-8)

Even in Sarojini's patriotic poems, there are some striking images. 'Gift of India' is a kind of homage to the heroic sons of India who sacrificed their lives in the First World War, fighting from the side of the Allies. They died unknown and unlamented on the foreign soil. There is a bunch of similes which throw up scintillating images:

Gathered like pearls in their alien graves
Silent the sleep by the Persian waves,
Scattered like shells on Egyptian sands,
They lie with pale brows and brave, broken hands
They are strewn like blossoms mown down by
chance
On the blood-brown meadows of Flanders and
France. (7-12)

The dead bodies of the great sons of India were gathered like pearls and consigned to alien graves. They lie in oblivion like the shells scattered on Egyptian stands, and again they are strewn 'like blossoms mown down by chance'. The images intensify the thematic appeal of the poem.

Sarojini in her use of simile and metaphor may appear, at times, quaint from the point of view of English rhetoric but it is quite natural to the traditional Indian sensibility and thought. Feeling, perception and imagination are blended here not into a line but into a unit of consciousness. An image in her poetry stands for a whole range of experience and vision. Her images are soft and delicate with feminine emphasis on colour and beauty. Armando Menezes in his brief portrait of Sarojini Naidu, finds the feminine sensibility in her poetry as it is reflected in her choice of passions, imagery and words: "And she had a woman's love of words. They were not, to her, just convenient instruments of expression, they were things: precious, lovely things, like jewels. She rejoices in polysyllables that roll and rumble, or rattle like long burnished swords: in phrases like 'lovely stalactite of dreams'; or 'in the long dread, incalculable hour.'" (46)

Sarojini's imagery and symbols confirm the fact that she is a poet of high poetic sensibility and imagination. Her poetry may not reflect seriously on life's intricacies but she definitely makes the scene look real in colours and tune, and they bespeak for her extraordinary range of imagery and symbols. A neo-modernist may regard her imagery merely fanciful but in so doing he forgets that she is a free singer.

Works Cited

Narvane, V.S. *Sarojini Naidu*. New Delhi: Orient Longman, 1980.

Naidu, Sarojini. *The Golden Threshold*. London: William Heinmann, 1905.

Naidu, Sarojini. *The Bird of Time.* London: William Heinmann, 1912.

Bush, Douglas. ed. *The Selected Poetry of Tennyson.* New York: The Modern Library, 1951.

Menezes, Armando. *Lighter Than Air.* Dharwar: Samyukta Karnataka Press, 1959.

7

Search for a Secular Imagination in A.K. Ramanujan

T. R. Joy

I

As a student of literature, I was taught to admire great writers. But quite often I found the very bad in the very best, and the very best in the very bad. Some of the masterpieces I have not understood myself. Later I wondered whether I should devote my time as a student and teacher of literature to admiration of their greatness and reverence for their position in the canon.

I think hero worship is an insult to adult human individuality and mature human dignity. The historical awareness about the injustice of the Divine Right for feudal domination, as we know, led to struggles for democracy at many levels. Even before the dawn of modern representative democracy, art and literature showed the signs of our sense of independence and freedom. They uphold our value for individuality and freedom.

Neverthless, the history of art and literature is one of warring trends and institutions of class, colour, race and gender. On the one hand, art and literature celebrate individuality and difference as their source and resource; on the other, these institutions do not seem to tolerate the inconvenience of openness and inclusion. For my part, approving of such institutional hegemony and their artistic and literary proclivities would be unjust. It would not encourage and empower a more constructive artistic and literary culture where the creativity and the dignity of the reader as well as of the writer are democratically sustained with mutual respect, communion and contribution. In fact, an open literary culture should empower us to discover and discern our creativity, not just genuflect before the genius of the masters.

Nagged as I was by these thoughts, when I read A.K. Ramanujan, I found his texts offer such an imaginative literary possibility and culture.

II

Creative and critical transgressions are fundamental to A.K. Ramanujan's work as a poet, translator, folklorist and scholar. The thematic and formal perspectives that his texts, sources and their contexts generate, point to a committed search for a secular and inclusive imagination. Ramanujan seems to imply that this secular imagination could become aesthetically productive and relevant, culturally just and open.

A secular imagination in poetry or literature should be considered in conjunction with the fundamental constituents of the literary phenomenon and process. That is to say:

- the life world/the worldview, which is the raw-material and source of literature;
- the authorial process, which is the human source and agency;
- the language/dialect, which is the fuzzy material, is medium as well as another kind of agency for literature;

- the reader response and process in his/her language; and lastly
- the work itself in its concrete or virtual linguistic and semantic condition problematically caught between the content and the form, the text and its context.

For the present and for brevity, I intend to focus mainly on the poetic works of A.K. Ramanujan with special reference to *The Black Hen* (1995)[1] and *Uncollected Poems and Prose* (2001)[2].

The imagination informing the source and core of Ramanujan's work is secular, democratic and inclusive, i.e., open to cultural and aesthetic heterodoxy in sensibility and practice. The thrust of such an imagination is relevant, when the value of a democratic order in society and in matters of art is increasingly under threat. The inquiry becomes also important in the context of the refusal of such a secular aesthetics in Ranjit Hoskote's introduction[3] to the Penguin anthology, *Reasons for Belonging: Fourteen Contemporary Indian Poets.*

After clarifying their pedigree, class, reputation, and allegiances, he has "chosen to focus on poets who recognise poetry as a *sacramental* rather than an instrumental use of language..."[4] The medievalism of the sacramental against the instrumental and the feudalism of a Brahminical/ clerical kind, justify the aesthetics of exclusion and formal purity. This reminds me of the way ecclesiastical politics uses systematic theology and spirituality to subvert and almost sabotage the responsible Christian practice in favour of rubrics and sacraments. The obsessive emphasis on the language of poetry privileges an exclusive vocation for the sacramental act in the "liberated zone"[5] of poetry, to quote Hoskote again, "the only real homeland that the poet can claim"[6], to escape from or ward off "the continuous war of positions that is contemporary life."[7] As against the aristocratic or oligarchic sacramentality of poetic imagination and process, Ramanujan seems to subscribe to a secular perspective. A general overview of his career and professional commitment shows his egalitarian temperament and taste. I call him a secularist for want of a better word more inclusive and democratic enough. In certain ways, I feel Ramanujan's creative and critical practices emerge from and are informed by a kind of friendly quarrel with the so-called mainstream *marga,* aesthetic insularity and purity.

III

Ramanujan concludes his essay on 'Classics Lost and Found'[8] with his own whole long poem, 'Prayers to Lord Murugan' from his second book, *Relations* (1971). This is important here. He does not try to sanitise or sanctify the so-called Indian traditions or ethos; rather he debunks the conventional notions of prayer as well as politics:

Lord of the sixth sense,
give us back
our five senses.

Lord of solutions,
teach us to dissolve
and not to drown.

Deliver us O presence
from proxies
and absences

from Sanskrit and the mythologies
of night and the several
roundtable mornings

of London and return
the future to what
it was.

This is an instance of secular imagination, as the poem subverts not only the conventional notion of prayer but also that of literary and cultural hegemonies symbolised in the expression, "from Sanskrit and the mythologies". The way he deliberately leaks his poetry into his academic paper making it essential to the structure as its conclusion, becomes an inclusive yoking together of the academic and the poetic, the sacred and the profane.

The same kind of creative and secular overlap precipitates in his poetry too. In his poem, 'Salamanders'[9] from *The Black Hen*, notions of nothing, zero, numbers and time mix easily and casually with sounds, words and metaphors as if they were regular fictional characters:

> Again, here it comes, the nothing,
> the zero where the numbers die or begin,
> the sunless day, the moonless month,
> where sounds do not become words
> nor words the rivals of silence.

This poem that commences like a Buddhist discourse on the very being of nothing shifts into the mythology of salamanders living "in fire" drinking "the flame" in the second section, and comes back to the very tactile and visual environment of ordinary lizards in the same sentence:

> ... but when I met
> them in the sludge of September
>
> woods after rain, they were ember -
> red but cold, born new and blind
> naked earthlings, poor yet satin
> to the eye, velvet to the touch.

Thereafter, the abstract and the concrete, the metaphoric and the metaphysical, the mythical and the mundane merge in the tropes of the historical to strike home the secular and contemporary charge of the poem: The cruel realities of our disturbing present history, violence and suffering that can doom our future. The poem disturbs us into the awareness of how myth and reality, superstition and science coagulate and coexist in us as "we burn/and eat fire no less than salamanders." It is interesting to note the way metaphysical and abstract notions are secularised by the dynamics of language and metaphor in the poem to achieve the effect of a dramatic interaction as if among fictional characters.

It is well known that Ramanujan has creatively recovered from our traditions a whole treasure of *Folktales from India*[10]. This again is another dimension of his commitment to a secular imagination and an egalitarian literary culture and sensibility. There are poems influenced and informed by Ramanujan's long years of research on and acquaintance with non-Sanskritic South Indian poetry and the alternative traditions of folklore. One wonderful instance of folklore and poetry tackling the *darshanic* question of death, common to all cultures and schools of thought, is the poem, 'Death in Search of a Comfortable Metaphor'.[11] Its figurative texture is woven by employing the story telling strategy of folktales. But, the narrative tapestry of this poem is transformed by visual, tactile and olfactory imagery and variety. In fact, the existential concern of death in the poem is brought down to earth even in the way language is used. The matter-of-fact but breathless burst of description of the life cycle of a scorpion in the second line of the second stanza, ending only at the close of the fourth stanza, the longest sentence in the poem, illustrates this point: A.K. Ramanujan religiously absolves the section of any sacred diction, subverts it again by the use of ironic mundane expressions, and above all, by the avoidance of any classical formal lineation devices. The only deviation can be the last line. Such a poetic process with its linguistic and figurative dynamics is charged by what I call a secular imagination. Let me quote the relevant section from the poem:

Maybe death is such
a scorpion: bursts its back
and gives birth
to numerous dying things,
baby scorpions,

terrifying intricate
beauties, interlocked
in male and female,
to eat, grow, sting,
multiply, burst their backs

in turn, and become feasts
of fodder for working
ants, humus for elephant
grasses that become elephants,
that leave their herds
to die grand lonely deaths.

Bruce King's observation in his revised edition of *Modern Indian Poetry in English* (2001) comes close to what a secular creative imagination would imply: "Ramanujan early rejected notions of spiritual transcendence; his poetry shows that reality is in the particular, the specific, the individual experience. The lesson he drew from both *Upanishads* and science was that after a life of unsatisfied fantasies and self-destructive passions we return to nature but as part of the food chain."[12]

Broadly speaking, Ramanujan's secular perspective welcomes other points of view, mainstream or not, as it searches for the ever-elusive core and possibilities of creativity. His work may not support an exclusive or exclusionary literary institution of masters and canons, which alone adjudicates the sanctity of the sacred domain of literature to save it from the pagan and profane contamination of the non-sacramental. Ramanujan seems to celebrate and establish the complex and often complicit sources and resources of creativity and poetry. The sublime and the earthy, the outstanding and the ordinary, the poetic and the prosaic, the tentative and the definitive - all can interface in the catalysing fertility of an open and inclusive secular imagination. The title poem, 'The Black Hen'[13] reveals the dialectics of the essential ambiguity and anxiety, the tenuous, this-worldliness undercutting the conventional sublime emergence of poetic expression.

It must come as leaves
to a tree
or not at all

yet it comes sometimes
as the black hen
with the red round eyes

on the embroidery
stitch by stitch
dropped and found again

and when it's all there
the black hen stares
with its round red eyes
and you're afraid.

If the first stanza refers to the spontaneous inspiration of the poetic genius, the second and third ones subvert the classical imperative, as it were, of an authentic poetic expression. All the same, Ramanujan recognises and leads the poem to the crucial element of the creative mystery where the fictional and the artistic merge with the real.

Now, I would like to focus on his poems about the creative process in his book, *Uncollected Poems and Prose,* to follow up the possibility towards Ramanujan's poetics as a secular way of creative engagement. Three poems may be undertaken in this context: 'Daily Drivel: a monologue', 'Figures of Disfigurement' and 'Children, Dreams, Theorems'.

'Daily Drivel: a monologue'[14] is a poem of 26 lines in free verse without stanza divisions. As the title suggests, it is in the conversational mode. The speaker of the poem talks to his/her friend who is absent. The major first section of the poem, seventeen and half lines to be precise, is about the speaker, almost breathlessly listing "how many things I did/ in the four hours you were gone": These "things" include humorous and mundane emergencies and errands like showing "my burning bottom to a young doctor", hobbling "back to do my laundry", visiting the gym and the grocery store, trying to "get my income tax returns postmarked", eating dinner, sending off "taxi receipts", washing "all my cups and saucers" and sitting down "for ten whole minutes/doing nothing."

It is at this point the other character in the poem 'you' is introduced in two and a half lines of the final sentence:

> ... But you went
> singlmindedly to see Othello
> deepening your sense of life,

The poet has used the conventional parameters of an elitist literary sophistication and its institutions supposed to cultivate the "sense of life" to counter its arguments. But those two and half lines accentuate the inadequacy of the so-called literary cultivation to sprout the harvest of a poem. Ramanujan works out the ironic charge and the implied disapproval of such a position in the following section that he allows tenuously to hang as a subordinate clause to the main one quoted above.

> *while I scattered my hours*
> *on the wind not even wishing*
> *they were precious seed*
> *that could sprout a harvest*
> *by springtime.*

He seems to discover in the actual process of writing

this poem, that the creative moment, a poem is born, could come from his scattered hours living and doing all those very ordinary things:

> and write this daily drivel
> which I hadn't done for a week.

The very term 'drivel' subverts the notion of poetry and the term in a way secularises the whole process of a poem. Moreover, the secularising impact of A.K. Ramanujan's imagination is emphasised by the conversational tone, spoken utterances, and the very mundane diction. Even the words like 'seed' and 'harvest', working metaphorically for poetic process connote a source and imagination much more secular in outlook than an institutionalised puritanical aesthetic.

In effect, this successful poem emerges from such non-incidents and everyday experience, and not from the sophisticated literary cultivation, symbolised in going to see *Othello*. In a way, similar poetic processes operate collectively or otherwise, in the formation of folktales and legends: The way they sprout, get talked about, edited, interpreted and altered for further versions and even new ones. This, in fact, points to a collective literary enterprise that slowly and steadily fosters a democratic literary culture and sensibility.

A subversion of the sacramental mystique of the romantic notions as well as the complementary critical assessment of poetic inspiration and genius is quite evident in his poem, 'Figures of Disfigurement'.[15] The very title is an ironic debunking of the literary pretension of conventional 'figures' that represents the technical devices specific to the process of poetry:

> *Epilepsy may confer*
> *powers of ecstasy*
> *sometimes; amnesia may*
> *open memories of past*

lives. Timely death
may give away a heart
or an eye.

Moreover, the poem deliberately blurs the spheres of the ordinary and the outstanding, the natural and the artistic, making the paradox of the title very valid in the context of the present discussion. Here Ramanujan seems to approve of the ancient Tamil poetics: "In contrast to Sanskrit", Ramanujan found, "early Tamil aesthetics makes no clear distinction between *bhava* and *rasa*, the raw everyday feelings and the refined emotions of art and poetry. If etymology means anything the native word for culture, '*panpu*', sometimes means nature, while in other contexts it connotes culture. *Pan* means 'to produce'; it also means 'a harmony, a musical mode'-- a complex of meaning, inclusive of both nature and culture: very different from Sanskrit *samskrta* which implies 'a refinement, a redoing' of things natural".[16]

Another typical process poem that exemplifies the play of Ramanujan's secular imagination at the thematic and formal levels is 'Children, Dreams, Theorems'.[17] The dominant nouns of the title humorously interact and interchange to converge into the complex artistic source and process of a poem. Here the conventions of punctuations and capitalisation are disregarded; the categories, concepts and concrete experiences like children, dreams, poems, theorems, quarrels, caressing, kissing, naming, talking and the like are all allowed to linguistically and metaphorically intersect and interact. The humorous and multilayered mechanics of such a poetic process, that Ramanujan aims at, can be summed up in these lines:

dreams like poems get lost
if their tails are not knotted
for memory

poems like my father's midnight

theorems get lost if you do not
talk to them, ...

get lost if you do not smell them
early and change their diapers
sprinkle talcum on their bottoms

How a scientific term like 'theorems' gets its bottom sprinkled by talcum! By the casual listing of poems, children, theorems, dreams, etc. with interchangeable attributes and responses Ramanujan has secularised not only the thematic concern of the poem but also its linguistic design to achieve a kind of dictional democracy, as it were.

Although there is no doubt about the "exquisite workmanship", the tactile and the visual quality of Ramanujan's poems,[18] he seldom accurately accommodates any well-established classical poetic forms and conventions. A.K. Mehrotra vouches for it when he finds that "Ramanujan generally gives a poem a shape that is original to it"[19] in his latest book, *An Illustrated History of Indian Literature in English* (2003). Vinay Dharwadkar in his Introduction to *The Collected Poems* recollects an incident where Ramanujan chose to go against the convention of long poems. He reports that the poet broke up "into fourteen relatively short poems". 'Elements of Composition' originally (1985) a "long poem of a few hundred lines arranged in about twenty-five sections".[20] Another of Mehrotra's observations is that "there is little doubt about the ways in which" Ramanujan's translations of the ancient Tamil poetry have "shaped his own English poems".[21] This reinforces his commitment to open up a heterodox literary culture and sensibility working out the vital connection between mainstream as well as marginalized genres and literatures. Bruce King reveals that "*The Collected Poems* Ramanujan was working on before his death was to include translations of his own writings in Kannada."[22]

IV

The secular imagination, that informs A. K. Ramanujan's poetry as well as his other works, does not disregard the sacred, the religious and other *marga* theories. Although he recognises the "crippling and not an enabling presence"[23] of Sanskrit, he strived towards a democratic ecosystem of aesthetics, which could encourage imagination, critical oppositions and creative contestations. In fact, one of his studies in his *Collected Essays*, "Some Thoughts on 'Non-Western' Classics: With Indian Examples",[24] Ramanujan has chosen to conclude it with a 12th century Sanskrit poem approving of its "recipe for a world literature", which only foregrounds the egalitarian and inclusive creative engagements Ramanujan also aspired for:

What a Poet Should Know

A poet should learn with his eyes
the forms of leaves
he should know how to make
people laugh when they are together
he should get to see
what they are really like
he should know about oceans and mountains
in themselves
and the sun and the moon and the stars
his mind should enter into the seasons
he should go
among many people
in many places
and learn their languages

Complementing the secular aesthetic concern of the above Sanskrit poem, I would like to keep alongside a 9th century Tamil poem, 'The Paradigm'[25] from Ramanujan's own translation of *Nammalvar.*

We here and that man, this man,
and that other in-between,
and that woman, this woman,
and that other, whoever,

those people, and these,
and these others in-between,
this thing, that thing,
and this other in-between, whichever,

all things dying, these things,
those things, those others in-between,
good things, bad things,
things that were, that will be,

being all of them,
he stands there.

I think the 'he' that "stands there" could really be the secular imagination of poetry breathing freely in such an inclusive creative climate and culture.

V

Still the question will remain: Can imagination be secular at all? The word 'secular' can become suspect because of its ideological and historical drag. But, 'secular' has an origin and history of dissent and inclusion on behalf of democracy, both in its western as well as Indian upbringing and evolution.

As we know, transgression belongs to the core and character of art and poetry. This quality is what has provoked and promoted most of the major artistic and literary trends and movements. And it is one of the most powerful impacts of art and literature on human mind. The very process of artistic defamiliarisation of the formalist variety too, generates its own transgressive force and justifies the poetic tendency to transcend the medium, break the barriers of formal rigidity.

So, 'secular' has shown its resilience to evolve with changing times and trends to become more inclusive and sufficiently critical. The use of 'secular' to modify 'imagination' does not diminish its possibility to be more creative; it allows imagination its ideological non-alignment and freedom to transcend artistic/literary parochialism. As a result, our imagination remains at its genetically valid neural complex, common to all. And that would help imagination excite and disturb us into a fertile ecosystem of poetic/artistic enterprises and critical responses. In short, this view of secular imagination would maintain the reality and the resilience of any literary work in its linguistic and semantic condition contentiously caught between the content and the form, the text and the context, as I have already hinted at in the introduction.

The strategy of 'win-win theory' of management was the realisation of the inadequacy of elitist, exclusionary, success-driven outlooks and practices. The emerging awareness of the need for equitable and just share of success and opportunity with a wider spectrum is essential to sustainability even in matters of economics and business. It is all the more relevant in the context of the plurality of the cultural and literary reality of India. The implied secular imaginative spectrum will not stop anybody from choosing to join the first order of sacramental aesthetic to dedicate oneself to its chaste objectives and sacred rubrics to strive for the holy grail of linguistic formal purity. We are supposedly in an age of collective creative enterprises as in filmmaking, television, art installations, interactive stage performances, cutting-edge research in science and technology and interdisciplinary research in the humanities. The concept of a secular imagination is relevant and significant as it becomes an inclusive but discerning antenna for creative and critical sensibility.

References

1. Ramanujan, A.K. *The Collected Poems of A.K. Ramanujan*. Delhi: Oxford University Press, 1995, pp.193-277.

2. Daniels-Ramanujan, Molly and Harrison, Keith. eds. *A.K. Ramanujan: Uncollected Poems and Prose*. New Delhi: Oxford University Press, 2001.
3. Hoskote, Ranjit. ed. *Reasons for Belonging: Fourteen Contemporary Indian Poets*. New Delhi: Viking, Penguin Books India, 2002, pp. xiii-xviii.
4. *Ibid*. p. xvii.
5. *Ibid*. p.xxvi.
6. *Ibid*. p.xxvi.
7. *Ibid*. p.xxvi.
8. Dharwadker, Vinay. ed. *The Collected Essays of A. K. Ramanujan*. New Delhi: Oxford University Press, 1999, pp. 184 -196.
9. Ramanujan, A.K. 1995, pp. 202-203.
10. Ramanujan, A.K. *Folktales from India: A Selection of Oral Tales from Twenty-two Languages*. New Delhi: Viking, Penguin Books India, 1993.
11. Ramanujan, A.K. 1995, p.273.
12. Bruce King , 2001, p. 299
13. Ramanujan, A.K. 1995, p. 195
14. Daniels-Ramanujan, Molly and Harrison, Keith. eds. 2001, p.25.
15. *Ibid*, p. 9.
16. Ramanujan, A.K. "Towards an Anthology of City Images". Dharwadker, Vinay. ed. *The Collected Essays of A.K. Ramanujan*. New Delhi: Oxford University Press, 1999, pp.71-72.
17. Daniels-Ramanujan, Molly and Harrison, Keith. eds. 2001, p.12.
18. Mehrotra, A.K. ed. 1992. *The Oxford Indian Anthology of 12 Modern Indian Poets*. New Delhi: Oxford University Press. pp.34-35.
19. Mehrotra, A.K. "Looking for A.K. Ramanujan". ed. Mehrotra, A. K. *An Illustrated History of Indian Literature in English*. Delhi: Permanent Black, 2003, p.300.
20. Ramanujan, A.K. 1996, p. xxxvii

21. Mehrotra, A.K. 2003, p. 299.
22. King, Bruce. 2001, p. 300
23. Dharwadker, Vinay. ed. 1999, p.192.
24. *Ibid.* pp.115-123.
25. *Ibid.* pp.120-121.

8

"Caries": A Discourse on Daruwalla's Construction of Discourse

Jayshree Goswami and *Mojibur Rahman*

The present paper intends to study the discourse construction of 'Caries'. This poem by Daruwalla has been interpreted on the discourse model provided by Halliday.

According to Halliday and many other functional linguists, anthropologists, sociologists as well as philosophers of language, language study cannot be successfully fulfilled without considering the situation of context, for it is constrained and influenced by the situation of context. These practitioners stress that the study of words, utterance even whole chunks of discourse, cannot be appreciated without the convention of contexts among them. Context can well be understood from Norman Fairclough's interpretation of discourse- "the ways of representing aspects of the world- the processes, relations and structures of the material world, the 'mental world' of thoughts, feelings, beliefs and so forth, and the social world." (124) In addition, Halliday claims that the context of situation is obtained through a systematic relationship between the social environments on the one hand, and the functional organization of language, on the other, which can be best understood in terms of "registers". Register, a semantic concept, is very important because it is seen as the linguistic consequence of interacting aspects of contexts, which Halliday calls "field, tenor and mode." These three contextual features help in constructing an idea about the texts' purposes and reasons, as well as its structure, and the adequate use of language in the text. 'Field' refers to the topics and actions which language is used to express; 'tenor' indicates the language users, their purposes, and their relationship to each other. 'Mode' stands for the channel through which communication is carried out.

Caries

(1) First when the teeth got caries
(2) they stuffed them with silver.
(3) The relief! Earlier even politicians
(4) as they talked to him
(5) took their hankeys to the nose!
(6) Now he didn't have to chew
(7) cloves or cumin seed
(8) or perfumed areca nut.
(9) He didn't have to daub his clothes
(10) with pungent perfumes of *kewra* or rose.
(11) For the manholes in his mouth were plugged.
(12) His own kisses were welcome now;
(13) the girls wanted more!
(14) Beyond the friction and the skin of sex
(15) he probed for feeling. It dawned on him
(16) that in the absence of stink, ideals
(17) are almost within reach. Fleeting aberration.
(18) Ideals always were at hand he discovered;
(19) you only had to reach for your pocket book!
(20) His half-truths had an edge over his rival's now.
(21) His clichés were backed by better amplifiers.
(22) His smile was more toothsome.

The people he bombarded with his grapeshot lies
were more vulnerable.
The election was already in his pocket!
Then it stank again.
Shards of mutton and decaying leaf
sawed away at the cutlery of the mouth
and caries came gunning
through the portholes of the gums.
This time, they said, we must
stuff the mouth with gold;
over the chasm we must build a bridge,
cap the front teeth with a gold crown
and wrap an enamel-skin around them
so that they look natural.
In the city his house remained as it was,
cows and goats tethered in front,
open drains flowing all around,
clogged with offal and spinach-leaf.
People must still think that he was
simple, one of them.
only in the bedroom air-conditioners hummed
and thick rugs covered it wall to wall.
And he started asking friends
"What are those swiss banks?
How the hell do they operate?"
He has enough now, but whenever the mouth is empty
the teeth go clack, clack, clack.
They are an appetite which has calcified
along the jawline.
Now it is not the mouth which stinks;
only hi swords,
like maggots from the body
Of overripe fruit.

(53-54)

Poem as Discourse

Field, tenor, and mode of the poem

In the poem 'caries', the field of the poem is expressed as verbal art. It represents the Indian socio-political scenario, which is unscrupulous and reprobate. The background and the predominant image, the speaker's mood, the relationship between the narrator and the protagonist form the sub-field.

The tenor is expressed through the relationship of the narrator with the character. In the poem, the relationship is expressed through the pronouns 'they' and 'he'. It indicates that the narrator does not share an intimate relationship, but as appears from his tone is cynical of the protagonist's acts. The purpose of the narrator is to unveil the true nature of the character. The poem exhibits the play between the appearance and the reality, and the narrator attempts to demonstrate this play being played by the Indian politicians.

The mode is expressed through the textual function. The poem is satirical which has a predominant image of caries. Moreover, the form adopted for communication is free verse.

Analysis of the poem

In the first stanza, the persona elicits an issue of caries. This noun, apart from upholding a denotative meaning, also functions at the connotative level. The noun exhibits an affiliation of the Indian political leader with the decayed human anatomy of teeth. The entire decayed mouth shares an implied relation with the Indian political system.

The discourse is in a narrative mode with instances of dialogue. The speaker or the third person narrator is an Indian citizen, who is aware of the contemporary Indian political scene. The discourse begins with a description of a past decayed, diseased state of teeth as denoted through the words "first when", and "earlier". Both these words have the feature {+ past} and at the same time it hints at an influential change later on. Further, the context or the situational background of the discourse is explicitly denoted through the noun "politician" (line 3), and "The election was already in his pocket!"(line 25). This is also because the expressions "Earlier even politicians" (line 3), "as they talked to him" (line 4), and "took their hankeys to the nose!" (line 5) denote the affinity of the character with the politicians. It is found that the discourse mentions an abnormal condition of teeth, as it is afflicted with caries. Nevertheless, what is worth examining is the remedy adopted to confront this diseased state. The character prefers stuffing the teeth with silver {+ornamentation, +deception} which results in "the relief!" The exclamatory expression hints at the success, and the immediate pleasure out of the deceptive act. Further, we notice that the household remedies like chewing of "cloves or cumin seed/ or perfumed areca nut." daubing clothes "with pungent perfumes of kewra or rose" hints at the Indian setting. So the politician belongs to India. There are certain lexical items in the fifth stanza which relate to the ideational meaning of caries. They are "manholes" (line 11), "stink (line 16), and "Fleeting aberration" (line 17). Similarly, there are also a set of lexical cohesive item that relates to the superficiality. They are "silver" (line 2), "perfumed areca nut" (line 8), "pungent perfumes" (line 10), "absence of stink" (line 16), and "Ideals always were at hand". (line 18) The gap between deception and reality, and the predominance of deceit over verity also hints at the gullibility and imbecility of the citizens as they fail to apprehend the real motive of the politician. The discourse intimates a shift of noun, from the noun caries to the noun manholes; from a small decay to a sewer. The shift signifies the intensity of corruption, degeneration, and contamination inherent in the character, as well as the system that advocates it. Thus, the character realizes:

> that in the absence of stink, ideals
> are almost within reach. Fleeting aberration.

Ideals always were at hand he discovered;
you only had to reach for your pocket book!

The entire discourse is an ironic realization of ideals by the character. Two expressions are contrasted here; they are "stink" and "ideals". This is something ironic as the narrator intends to present a view that is not acceptable in the normal code of conduct. What is unacceptable is the equation of "absence of stink" with the realization of ideals. The narrator seems to be cynical of the character's attitude in "Ideals always were at hand he discovered; / you only had to reach for your pocket book!" Associating ideals {+grand} with pocket book {-grand} conveys the lowliness and commercialization of these ideals.

In the next stanza, the narrator depicts the activities of the character after he has acquired sham to hide his genuine nature. The outcomes of his trickery are:

His half-truths had an edge over his rival's now.
His clichés were backed by better amplifiers.
His smile was more toothsome.
The people he bombarded with his grapeshot lies
were more vulnerable.
The election was already in his pocket!

The force and urgency in the tone suggests the urgency and intensity of the actions. The words like "rivals", "amplifiers", "bombarded", "grapeshot", and "vulnerable" relates to the ideational meaning of "violence", therefore, suggestive of the violence adopted for winning the election. Apart from violence he also takes recourse to half-truths like smile and lies {+false} that resulted in apparent accomplishment of his goal- "the election was already in his pocket!"

To begin the third stanza it is commendable referring to a comment of the narrator in the first stanza, which is "Fleeting aberration". Therefore, the third stanza bespeaks of the failure. It is because the true self "came gunning". Like in the first stanza, in the third stanza too, there are many lexical cohesive items related to caries. These are "shards of mutton and decaying leaves" as well as "carries came gunning". This time silver was not adequate, so a change is required, a change that was suggested in the first stanza:

> This time, they said, we must
> Stuff the mouth with gold;

There is a shift in the time sequence. From the past description of the actions the focus shifts to the present, along with an emphasis on the modal verb "must". The use of this modal indicates that stuffing teeth with gold is a necessity. Gold {+ ornamentation} is a cohesive item that shares affinity with silver (1st stanza), though gold is esteemed for a higher value than silver. Nevertheless, the meaning of gold deviates from the usual code, and attains a specific meaning in the context. In this stanza gold signifies that the character should put up a mask of honesty, honour, and dependability, so that he can appeal to the masses.

> over the chasm we must build a bridge,
> cap the front teeth with a gold crown
> and wrap an enamel-skin around them
> so that they look natural

The entire discourse intimates dissimulation. In order to hide his pernicious and fallacious deeds the leader cloaks his acts with gold or falsehood. Building a bridge over the chasm suggests that the differences between the leader and the populace should be resolved. Furthermore, in order to make his guile look natural he must wrap an enamel skin {+ natural} for restoring the natural colour of teeth, or the cordial relationship. What is significant is the pronoun "we", as it indicates the involvement of not one leader, but of many.

Lexical items in a discourse as a chain can link paragraphs or stanzas closely and tightly. The lexical items really as a chain play a key role in connecting the first stanza with the second, third, and the fourth stanza of this poem together in a cohesive order with logical ideational meaning. It also connects the fifth stanza skillfully. In the fifth stanza, the narrator describes further falsehood. The dichotomy between truth and falsehood generates irony in the stanza and the duality in public and private life denotes the hypocrisy of the character. The character maintains a projected self:

> In the city his house remained as it was,
> cows and goats tethered in front,
> open drains flowing all around,
> clogged with offal and spinach-leaf.
> People must still think that he was
> simple, one of them

The character adopts the dingy and decayed lifestyle to make his self look more natural. Once again, there is a switch in the tense from present to the past. This is to evince the present change and contrast. The dull scenes {+ decay} like "open drains flowing all around", "clogged with offal", and "spinach-leaf" shares cohesive affinity with the carries. The belief "people must still think that he was/ simple, one of them" is a sarcastic comment on the gullibility of the citizens, who fail to distinguish between right and wrong, appearance and reality, and good and bad. The word "still" further enhances the sarcasm and at the same time denotes that they have been deceived in the past, is still being deceived, and will further be deceived in the future. Next, the ironical character sketch is made subtle by contrasting the earlier deplorable images with the modern comforts. Thereafter, reconstructing the thematic play between reality and illusion:

> only in the bedroom air-conditioners hummed

> and thick rugs covered it wall to wall.
> And he started asking friends
> "What are those swiss banks?
> How the hell do they operate?"

The first two lines share the semantic parallelism with the play between gold/ silver and the carries. The concealing of the air conditioners {+luxury} with the thick rags {+poverty} re- exemplifies the deception. The dialogue "what are those Swiss banks?/ how the hell do they operate?" relate to the contemporary socio-political situation of India where the dishonest industrialists, scandalous politicians, and corrupt IAS, IRS, IPS officers have deposited in foreign banks in their illegal personal accounts a sum of about $ 1500 billion, which have been misappropriated by them. This amount is about 13 times larger than the country's foreign debt. The reality is that the Indian economy has been stripped of its wealth.

The speaker's last comment on the character is worth examining. The comment brings out the true picture, the attitude, and the perception of the leader as the following lines suggest:

> He has enough now, but whenever the mouth is empty
> the teeth go clack, clack, clack.

The words "enough" and "now" relate to the success achieved by the leaders. The need for money and luxuries is exhibited in the statement "whenever the mouth is empty/ the teeth go clack, clack, clack." The reference to the teeth "as an appetite which has calcified" denotes the unaccounted money and the associated greed of the leaders. The persona ends his final comment with a dilapidated image:

> Now it is not the mouth which stinks;
> only his words,

like maggots from the body
Of overripe fruit.

Conclusion

The poem illustrates the prevailing corruption and the loopholes in the political system that on one hand facilitates the prosperity of the leaders and the deplorability of the nation on the other. There is no direct reference to any one political leader but an implied reference to all the criminals, dishonest, and debased men who use guile to win the faith of the citizens. The duplicity and guile, which resonates in all the stanzas, are referred through the cohesive items along with the images associated with the noun "caries". They anticipate and exhibit the decay and debris. The mode of discourse helps in demonstrating the satire as well.

Works cited

Fairclough, Norman. *Analyzing Discourse- Textual Analysis for Social Research.* Oxon: Routledge, 2003.

Daruwalla, Keki ·N. *Winter Poems.* Bombay: Allied Publishers, 1980.

Widdowson, H.G. *Stylistics and the Teaching of Literature.* Britain: Longman, 1975.

Mills, Sara. *Discourse.* London: Routledge, 2007.

Halliday, M. A. K. *An Introduction to Functional Grammar.* London: Arnold, 1985.

9

Eroticism in the Poetry of Shiv K. Kumar

Jindagi Kumari and *Rajni Singh*

Shiv K. Kumar is an illustrious name in the domain of Indian English Poetry. Emphasizing on the fact that contradictions involve every aspect of life, the poet outlines various stages of an individual's development. In the process, he records that psycho sexual response of humans are often contrasted to social values. The poet depicts human beings' entanglement into relationship of love and sex, and evinces their inability to overcome corruption and hypocrisy at different levels. Also, he draws on the sufferings caused by the anticipation of old age and death. However, the argument that surfaces Kumar's poetic body is - relationship, particularly man woman relationship. The poet presents the issue with a view to the various related aspects such as physical charm of woman, marriage, betrayal, divorce, loss of vigour etc. It is here that the poet finds a scope for the induction of erotic in his poetry and exploits his observance of responses and thoughts relating to sexual activity. The depiction of erotic in the poet, nevertheless, is not an end in itself but is used as a basis to understand human relationship and human nature at large. As mentioned previously, the poet eviscerates on eroticism while dealing with the themes of feminine charm, marriage, betrayal, divorce and aging. The study concentrates on the delineation of the eroticism in the poet's depiction of feminine enamour.

The word "erotic" is concerned with the arousal and satisfaction of sexual desire and its study involves the varied aspects of sexual or amatory love.[1] Erotic is derived from the Greek term Eros, basically referring to the love god that suggests a communication of both the sexes and is based on the pleasure principle. However, various mythical representations associate Eros at once to pleasure, achievement, success, pain, dissatisfaction, and an eternal quest. The term is also explained as linked to the creative aspect of life.[2]

In Indian context, Kama seems to be the nearest counterpart of Eros. Kama, the god of love in Hindu Mythology, symbolizes the significance of sexual love in life as an indispensable creative force which encompasses pleasure of union and creation. One finds that arousal of certain emotions enforces one to form a communion and express the blissful state of existence that have been basic to human nature. Nevertheless, the desire called eros is far from simple and has been rightly interpreted as involving a complex of emotions by Anne Carson:

> Simultaneous pleasure and pain are its symptom. Lack is its fundamental animating constituent. As syntax it impresse(s) us as something of a subterfuge: properly a noun, eros acts everywhere like a verb. Its action is to reach, and the reach of desire involves every lover in an activity of the imagination.[3]

Here, "Lack" as mentioned by Carson reminds one of the Lacanian "lack" where the psychoanalyst critic finds lack crucial for the arousal of certain wishes for the attainment of the desired object.

Coming to Indian context, the earliest possible reference

to sex act is made in the Rig-Veda where origin of sex is combined with the origin of "Mann", a free and active power centre that emerged from a sap that was spread all around at the time of the creation of the universe; together with "Mann" "Kama" originated; this idea is encapsulated in the following shloka:

> Kamastdagre' samawartatadhi manso retah prathamam tadasit.
>
> (Tiwary 7)

Brihadaranyak Upanisad says "Kammayam ewayam purushah" and *Eetareya Upanishad* considers sex as the light of the sweet wishes of Brahma or the Supreme Being. *Shatpath Brahman* has it that Prajapati, the creator of the world was single in the beginning but in this solitary life he felt acute loneliness. He desired the other and divided himself into two. Thus there happened husband and wife both part of a single self; separated from each other they are just a half.[4] (emphasis mine)

Besides scriptures, erotic has also been a recurrent theme of ancient Indian literature. Kalidasa's poetry has erotic elements interwoven with the description of the beauty of women, union and separation of lovers and other issues as well. The tradition continued with Bhartrihari's *Sringarasataka,* Amaru's *Amarusatak,* Jayadeva's *Gitagovinda,* Vidyapati's *Padavali,* and Vatsyayan's *Kamasutra,* the ancient Indian erotic manuals, that view sex with the pleasure principle at the centre. The text explicitly analyses erotic situation and gives a detailed description of the eccentric sex position and depicts the frank and voluptuous play of bodies that has a sole end of make-time-for-intimacy when other pressures are mounting.[5]

Also the sculpture, on the earliest temples- Konark, Saunak (near Baroda) and many others show that Indian art and architect had never been devoid of eroticism, rather sex worship and graphic representation of the union between man and woman has been a recurring feature. Even the very concept of 'lingam of the God Shiva resting in the centre of the yoni is in a way a representation of the art of creation, the union of Prakriti and Purush.'[7] (emphasis mine) Nevertheless, the ultimate essence of the work of ancient Indian erotic has always given a religious and spiritual bent simultaneously.

In the similar vein, 'Song of Songs' in *the Bible*, which is said to be one of the greatest pieces of erotic literature consisting of the acute representation of carnal love, description of epicurean beauty of lovers and their pining for each other. An instance is the following excerpt: "Thy navel is like round goblet, which wanteth not liquor. Thy belly is like a heap of wheat set about with lilies."[7]

However, art at present time has come of an age; the modern art theories, be it naturalism or abstract expressionism, derive their power from the artist's emotional connection to his perceptual reality underlying greater personal freedom.

With the emergence and prevalence of modern thoughts, portrayal of nude in art is no more reckoned as exorbitant or freakish. Nevertheless, erotic literature has always been viewed skeptically. The doubtful reception to erotic literature owes to its nature that seems to be overlapping with pornographic. Though, at times it becomes difficult to distinguish erotic from pornographic. It is said that pornography is always sexually explicit; it is not necessarily sexually arousing nor is pornography genuinely interested in artistic merit. Further, good quality eroticism, in contrast to pornography, is normally less sexually explicit and always sexually arousing. Eroticism is more artistic than pornography in capturing the beauty, shape and form of the human body and its deeper portrayal of our emotions, lust and desire. Erotic art portrays healthy sexuality and sex; which is joyful, exciting, intimate, interesting and pleasurable.[8] (emphasis mine)

Viewed in this background, Indian English Poetry lacks any such trend of erotica. However, induction of erotic element is observed in Tagore's love poems. Eroticism in Indian English Poetry began to be acknowledged in its explicitness in Ezekiel. However, it was only with Kamala Das's work that it could get its firm ground in the field. Now the trend thrives with a number of male and female poets such as Shiv K Kumar, Eunice De Souza, R K Singh, Meena Alexander, Mani Rao, Anuradha Nalapet, Vijaya Goel, Jayshree Loba, Prabha Mehta, and some others.

Shiv K. Kumar reflects the change in the attitude towards the reception of eroticism in the poem 'Adam to God', in terms of change in language and style:

> I guess I am speaking a new language not
> ... to communicate
> through fruit and flower,...
> If we stand here before you
> camouflaged by fig leaves, it's because of
> the fear of full exposure of body and mind.

The poets and artists of modern age prefer a new language that is the language of body and provide full exposure "of body and mind" to express both their pain and joy through it. The poet in the lines, thus, seems to justify the treatment of sex and sexuality in his work.

Depiction of female body and beauty has been an important aspect of erotic. Shiv K. Kumar presents this in nearly a dozen of his poems. The poems in this group include 'The Face' (*Articulate Silences*)[9], 'To a Young Wife' (*Cobwebs in the Sun* 2)[10], 'Indian Women' (4), 'An Indian Mango Vendor' (30), 'A Young Female Jogger' (*Trapfalls in the Sky* 55)[11], 'Birth of Eve' (71), 'Young Maidservant' (*Woodpeckers* 29)[12], 'To a Young Beautiful Woman Aspiring to be a Poet' (*Woolgathering* 48)[13], 'Lolita' (66), 'Voices at Night' (16), 'The Sea from A Cottage on the Beach' (*Thus Spake the Budhha: Poems* 35)[14], and 'Adam to God' (*Losing My Way: Poems* 7)[15] etc. In each of these poems the poet evokes eroticism by describing the bodily charm of woman that leads to love/sex and also exposes different outlooks related to the same. An instance is the poem 'The Face' where the lover seems to seek a communion with his beloved as he says: "Let your face arc over mine". (The Face 1) In the process of closeness he describes the physical contours of the lady who has got: "two scythed curls", "mole on", "left cheek", "tulipped mouth". These expressions, that otherwise contain sensuous appeal, when read in the context, are expressive of sheer sensuality devoid of any warmth in the communion. Remarkably, the features of beauty are presented with an association to highly academic and philosophical allusions, for example: "two scythed curls/ poised defiantly" (The Face 6-7) appear to the speaker enacting "Hegelian Dialectic— theses antitheses". Here, one finds the allusions to the Hegel's idea of thesis-antithesis or mutual pull between the two opposite forces which is used to illustrate the basic fact of the attraction between sexes. Further, the poet draws a contrast between the beauty of his beloved and the exemplary beauty of Helen of Troy by the following allusion:

> This is the face that launches
> a thousand paper-boats
> down my blood stream. (22-24)

These lines imply the sensual appeal of the woman contrasting it to the sensuousness of Helen that had far greater an impact as she proved to be the reason behind the launching of thousands of ships whereas, the lover of the speaker, probably a modern lady, could just be able to evoke limited impact on physical level signified as launching of "paper-boats" in his "blood stream".

However, one finds a different picture in the poem 'To a Young Wife' where, the speaker is mesmerized by the perception of the nude beauty of his beloved wife and considers his physical urge would be violating the beauty, therefore, discards the idea even after being strongly aroused, and the poet puts it thus:

Arabian horses
snort around our bed
pawing into frosted holes. (1-3)

The image of 'Arabian horses' is highly evocative and suggestive of masculine physical urge. And 'snort around our bed' is again suggestive of powerful sexual desire. Nevertheless, 'pawing into frosted holes' signifies the pacification of the drive. The speaker finds his beloved's body as beautiful as the Venus of Botticelli and is so carried away by the vision of beauty that he feels reluctant 'to act' and considers 'Deed' as 'perdition'.

Here, nudity is treated as an elevating element and the speaker seems to follow the maxim 'beauty is to see not to touch' lest the sanctity of it gets violated.

In contrast, in the poem 'Indian Women' the poet describes of physical excellences of Indian women combining it with the reflection on their desire, expectancy, and suffering that give the erotic a greater depth. The following lines show how Indian women endure the infliction caused by desires:

Patiently they sit
like empty pitchers
on the mouth of the village well... (4-6)

Here, 'empty pitchers' is suggestive of women who are sexually starved and suffer an eternal pang of separation in absence of their husbands.

Pleating hope in each braid
            of their Mississippi-long hair
            looking deep into the water's mirror
for the moisture in their eyes. (7-10)

The images in the above lines reflect the magnitude of hopefulness which makes them 'guard their tattooed thighs' (12) till their death. Here, guarding of 'tattooed thighs' suggests self restrictive approach to sex, which the poet at once seems to criticize and commend.

In another poem 'Young Maidservant' one finds the speaker captivated by the charms of his young maidservant. He observes her body and movement that stir his instinct:

> A mere smile can be a ritual
> and a frank swivel of the hips
> send gazelles capering
> through infinite space. (10-13)

Here, the speaker acknowledges his impulses that are overwhelmed by the charm of his maid servant as he notices her 'smile' and 'frank swivel of hips. The speaker is greatly incited; however he finds the maid 'the other moon' which is 'only three constellations away.' The phrase ironically implies the great distance created by social restriction. However, no value can be able to curb the arousal of desire; the persona expresses his urge to 'feel the tenderness of larks' that is to have a communion with his maid. The wish of the speaker emerges due to disappointed marital life and dissatisfied sex. The idea is present in the lines: "...knead the dough of wedlock/on sullen evening." (15-16) The loneliness and rejection of the speaker by his wife underlies the origin of his desire for 'the other'. Here, one notices that the imagery such as 'gazelles' and 'moon' which the poet has used for depicting female charm is of conventional type. However, these are joined with novel images like 'frank swivel of hips' and 'capering through infinite space' which are able to create a fresh appeal.

Another poem 'A Young Female Jogger' creates great erotic appeal. The poem describes the bodily movement and postures of a young female jogger as observed by the stealthy speaker who is stupefied by a sudden glimpse of the jogger. He portrays her as:

> Thor in your eyes
> flambeaux in your hair
> gazelles in your feet. (5-7)

The speaker perceives 'Thor' or a hammering emblematic of thunderbolt in the eyes of the jogger; he finds 'flambeaux' that is a flaming torch in her hair and movement of antelope in her feet. This appearance of woman is suggestive of aggressiveness, force and vigour which are the qualities generally associated with men. The image of woman is nevertheless, appealing to the eyes and overwhelms the sense of vision by its radiant eyes and dazzling hair. Moreover, the speaker finds in her 'a flying angel from Sistine' and decides to throw himself in her path 'to ask a boon' of her. However, the speaker realizes his inability as he says:

> But the doves of your breasts
> leaving a trail of eau de jasmine...
> ... charged to outfly the fawn. (12-16)

Realizing his limitation, the speaker takes recourse to speculation and imagination:

> If hips, thighs and calves sway to
> some rhythm, it must be a sort of
> love-play that knows how to leap across
> a pot-hole in the side-walk, an arc of the sky
> and also swing in bed. (17-21)

The minute observation of the movements of the jogger provokes the speaker to cogitate the possibilities to have a physical contact with the lady. The mention of the parts of the body- 'hips', 'thighs' and 'calves' provides the concrete image of the lady whereas expressions like 'a pot hole', 'an arc of the sky', 'swing in the bed leap across' are suggestive of sex act. Lastly, the speaker gives in, wondering the fortune of imaginary rival who awaits the jogger 'at the track's end.' He again takes recourse to anticipation and imagination:

> Will he mate you steel upon flint
> or just go down on his knees
> for a spurt of nectar
> from your navel? (23-26)

Here reference of mating 'steel upon flint' is highly erotic but at the same time very implicit. The speaker anticipates different ways of sexual communion with the lady. Like in the above lines, most often erotic in Kumar remains quite suggestive, nevertheless, not less appealing. In this context one feels tempted to quote Nietzsche's view on beauty:

> The noblest kind of beauty is that which does not transport us suddenly, which does not make stormy and intoxicating impressions but that which slowly filters into our minds.[16]

To conclude, one finds a nice blend of explicitness and suggestiveness in the presentation of erotic in the poems of Kumar. The most remarkable thing about erotic poems of Kumar is his honesty in depiction of erotic situation and his artistry in use of erotic expressions. The poet often puts forth primitive/instinctive drives of his speakers in the context of female beauty and gives us an opportunity to understand the human mind and situation.

So far as the image of a woman is concerned, he presents it in different lights. Though in every case they are represented as charming and attractive, the image is never portrayed just for the sake of evoking their beauty and charm merely for the delight of its presentation; there is always an implied purpose and function that is to express man's reaction to this charm, thereby examine his nature as a whole. However, in no way the function mars the sensuous appeal of aesthetics of erotic in the poems.

In his depiction of feminine beauty and charm Kumar

equally draws upon Indian imagery and symbols as well as allusion to western myths. At once he compares their movement with that of 'gazelle', and their beauty with 'moon' and finds in them 'Boticelli's Venus' and in their hair length of 'Mississippi'.

Moreover, women or females that the poet talks about are not distinguished figures; they are the common ladies; beloveds, wives, maidservants, joggers that one sees around in day to day life.

The erotic poems of Shiv K Kumar seem to be highly appealing. The expressions carry sensuous effect along with them, as they are combined with refreshing, radical and unique imagination. The poems stir our sense of vision, touch and smell but most importantly, they involve us in situations to be thoughtful. Kumar's is a pure erotic poetry replete with arousing effect, artistry, literary bent and situations helping us out to understand the basic human nature. Erotic consciousness in Kumar is, thus, instrumental to filter his vision of life.

References

1. (http://www.chacha.com/questions/what_does_erotic_mean) 24july 2009
2. http://www.etymonline.com/index.php?term=Eros21 August, 2009
3. (Quoted in) Moser, Thomas. C. A *Cosmos of Desire.*

   http://books.google.co.in/books?id=ooGfibUuYjsc&pg15[th] July
4. Tiwary, Ramashankar. 'Preface', *Soor ki Sringar Bhavana.* Delhi: Parimal Publications, 1999.
5. Deepa Menon."Kamasutra, Still on Top". *Femina.* August 12, 2009.
6. http://syedmdasadullah.blogspot.com/2009/07/nudity-isnt-obscenity-its-just-art.html.6march2010
7. http://www.gardenenclosed.com/index.html Aug 15 2009
8. http://www.spaceadmotion.com/erotic_literature.htm

9. Kumar, Shiv K. *Articulate Silences*. Calcutta: Writers Workshop, 1970.

10. ________. *Cobwebs in the Sun*. New Delhi: Tata Macgraw-Hill, 1974.

11. ________. *Trapfalls in the Sky*. Madras: Macmillan India Limited, 1986.

12. ________. *Woodpeckers*. London: Sidgwick &Jackson, 1979.

13. ________. *Woolgathering*. Mumbai: Disha Books, 1998.

14. ________. *Thus Spake the Buddha*. New Delhi: UBSPD, 2002.

15. ________. *Losing My Way: Poems*. New Delhi: Peacock Books, 2008.

16. http://www.spaceandmotion.com/Philosophy-Friedrich-Nietzsche- Philosopher.htm 6 march 2010.

10

Unvoiced Sorrow in the Poetry of Jayanta Mahapatra

Dinesh Panwar

The male dominated world in Orissa believes the emancipation of a woman, only within the parameters of patriarchal structures. Though the feminist writer claims that 'women are one half of the sky' but history witnesses anguish and agony of the woman. A woman has never been more than a sexual object in the eyes of a chauvinistic man. They have been kept away from basic needs and fundamental rights, and their worlds have been confined to home and kitchen. They have been merely treated as an object of sensual satisfaction. According to Kristeva: "By 'woman'. I mean that which cannot be represented, what is not said, what remains above and beyond nomenclatures and ideologies." [1]

We have plenty of feminist theories postulated by various authors and critics. They aim at ensuring egalitarianism of opportunities and rights for women in all sphere of life. Elizabeth Barret Browning, a Victorian poetess, who said in 1845, "England has had many learned women ..... and yet where are the poetesses? .... and I look everywhere for grandmothers and see none."[2] The practical application of feminist theories can be best illustrated through George Eliot's *Middle March*. Victorian morality made it difficult for Marian Evans to authenticate a fair justice for her work if she projected herself as a woman writer. So, she wrote under male pseudonym George Eliot to ensure the legitimacy and authority essential for her work. Mary Wollstonecraft's *A Vindication of the Rights of Woman* reiterates that the education of woman is only way to exonerate them from enslavement. Virginia Woolf's *A Room for One's Own* emphasizes economic independence and privacy for women. Simone de Beauvoir's *The Second Sex* criticizes subordination and alienation of women by the myth 'Woman is Man's Other'. Elaine Showalter's Feminist Criticism *In the Wilderness* admonishes the muted culture of women and the dominant culture of men. Kamala Das is a 'representative' of contemporary Indian feminist concerns. Her demand is to sink cultural difference such as region, religion and class. Her poem, 'An Introduction' is an archetypal symbol of woman's predicament.

Above mentioned are female authors and their raising of voice for women is natural. Jayant Mahapatra has also highlighted the pathetic conditions of women in his poetry. The sense of presenting the realities of a woman's life has always been sensible and significant. Mahapatra describes the cultural and spatial dispersion in the society. It means that there cannot be a singular cultural matrix in the cumulative tradition like that of Orissa. This form of dispersion creates space, and with the passage of time, the space becomes a troublesome phenomenon for existence. Gradually every individual starts understanding their role in the matrix of tradition. As they play their roles to achieve their required space they become victims of powerful one. A sustained tradition, like that of Orissa, draws a quest inward to the individual. The resultant quest thus becomes fiercely responsive to its socio- cultural reality. Mahapatra's creative works de-centered identity to speak about the space that a woman in the society deserves. The plight of women is a part and parcel of his poetry and it captures chunk of his theme. He delineates them in all shapes and figures. Mahapatra has a great reverence and veneration for women who are primordial symbol of suffering and sacrifice. In the words of Lucy Irigaray, the role that the woman has in the society "represents a sense of place for man" which means that she is nothing better than an object. She finds herself defined as a thing."[3] Mahapatra also confides in mythical saying, "Wherever women are revered God dwells there." But, at the same time, he is profoundly perplexed at perpetual and perennial problem pertaining to women. He discloses his disappointment and disgruntlement in this way:

> Perhaps, the status of the Indian women in our society today has gone down. It is pathetic indeed to read accounts of the degradation of our women subjected to in the daily newspapers. Cases of rape, murder, mutilation continue to fill the pages, and one sits helplessly, feeling this pain one is not able to do anything about.....I can see the pain in the eyes of women as they pass by the road every day; ... seems to say: we are the beast of the burden, like cattle. It is about this pain I would like to write because I can't do anything else.[4]

Mahapatra not only talks about these ostracized women but in general he describes the condition of women who are exiled at home. He uses a sad and serene voice to give their thought a narration. They are the sufferer in a relationship. Whether a wife, daughter, or a mother, the male dominated world has deprecated the limits of existence for the women. The role of wife is enunciated with speculative irony. The wife is alienated from the freedom that she enjoyed before marriage. Though we may be devout devotees of women divinities but when it comes to assisting 'the damsels in distress' and desolation we deter ourselves from our deeds. What to speak of common women, we do not spare even the Goddess Sita from passing through ordeal and severe trial where she is asked by husband Lord Rama to pass the "Agni Pariksha" to prove her chastity after she is released from abduction by the great monster Ravana. Draupdi, the wife of five Pandavas, is disrobed by Dushasana in the presence of all courtiers and stalwarts. We have copious example of such extent in our history and myth. And same is the plight of ordinary women in their conventional and customary lives. Mahapatra presents pen portrait position of Indian women:

> Surrounded by the rough noose
> of ownership, to feel
> A sort of dutifulness
> in the quiet bait of blood;
> frightened, frail of paper
> like an origami crane in the wind.
> While the man says:
> it's the same story. The same one
> we've heard a thousand times.

Women are acute sufferers of gender biasing. They are neglected and marginalized at both cultural and biological levels. At the one hand their life is restricted to house and kitchen, to look after the children, husband and others; on the other hand they are only meant to quench the carnal crave of men. Basically it is very painful that woman is compelled to be alone. She suffers from loneliness, not only a social one, but also an emotional loneliness. Mahapatra tries to describe this solitude with truth and authenticity. He succinctly sums up deploring and muted state of Indian women in the poem 'Dawn':

> There is a dawn which travels alone,
> Without the effort of creation, without puzzle.
> It stands simply, framed in the door, white in the air:
> Waiting for what the world will only let her do.

The news of most secret is made open secret. There is no privacy and secrecy for women. The state of attaining puberty and adolescence is celebrated with fabulous festivities and fanfares. Let the whole world know that a girl of sweet-sixteen is ripened in her sexuality and sensuality. Mahapatra's astonishment appears in this way:

> Two aunts, a distant cousin
> like a ghost of her disapproving mother,
> their genial grins as though redeemed
> by unchanging village ways
> mouths scarlet with paan juice,
> they recite tales
> to the glowing limbs of Chelammal....

Mahapatra presents pulchritudinous portrait of women struggling for their identity. They lead a meaningless and futile life. There is nothing but darkness all around them. The life is a living hell for them and they are bound to survive amidst sorrows and difficulties. They are mired in the mud of this mundane mayhem:

> In the darkened room
> a woman
> cannot find her reflection in the mirror
> waiting as usual
> at the edge of sleep
> In her hands she holds
> the oil lamp
> whose drunken yellow flames
> know where her lonely body hides.

Above listed lines are possibly maiden of Mahapatra's poetic career and he gave them title of 'A Missing Person'. It is autographical in tone and temperament. The intention and context of writing this poem is further corroborated by his conversation with authoress Neeru Tandon. The poet clarifies:

> "Married woman doesn't see her image in the mirror, when she looks she cannot find her features. Yes, it is loss of identity. A man was used to come drunk and; here of course I have taken it from a real incident, he used to beat his wife in front of me; I mean it happened in my house. I had a cousin who used to come late in the evenings and I would open the door because I was there; he would come and beat his wife; I saw it as a mere spectator, so these things affected me".[5]

The word 'women' is considered as a metaphor of sacrifice and suffering. Their desire and fate is destined by men. They are compelled to surrender against willful and stubborn desire of men. Mahapatra observes:

> And the women
> not answering to their names any more
> and usually lying like unexpected lakes
> deep within the wooded hills
> break their calm surfaces
> like wild water snakes
> let loose from the yearly floods

We have another example of woman being treated as a device of sex. In this regard comment of Madhusudan Prasad is plausible: "woman who is helpless and, therefore, eternally, 'Each night' exploited as a sex object by man to bury his 'hurt' inside her."[6] In the poem 'Idyll' Mahapatra writes:

> And something in a woman's eyes tempts confessions
> From her husband as they stretch out to sleep.
> A time never lost, rising as a mist, that floats upon consciousness;

Women feel insecure and unsafe away from home.

Wherever they go, evil and vulgar eyes of men stare at their sensuous limbs. They confront indecent and indecorous truant of men at public and non-public places. Mahapatra illustrates an instance of a shopkeeper staring in a lecherous way at woman who goes to shop to purchase four kilo of rice:

> Two big-arsed
> Srikakulam women
> nude hunger in eyes
> fans himself in the lethargy of his dream.

Mahapatra's soul is seriously shattered at the misery of women. They make their presence felt even in their absence and they remain to resonate and reverberate in his rhythmic rhyme. He aptly recapitulates:

> Even
> When she is
> Even
> When she is not

But about above lines different critics have different opinions as S. K. Desai comments:

> Nothing clearly emerges for the two clauses without complements, one positive and the other negative. It is the parallelism of the clauses, along with the semantic linking of woman. 'She' and 'she' that create some teasing ripples of floating feelings without substance. [7]

The following lines of the poem 'The Stranger My Daughter' deserve avid reading and multiple interpretations:

> My precious golden daughter
> looks out through the glass
> I nail two damp eyes to the door

and the while
the waiting draws me down
Drums beating under the earth
tremble her taut skin
there is a sun we know of
there are
the secret spasms to reason
Juices from my daughter's body
are filling the noisy hives

To start with, the poem is an another example of encroachment on the freedom of women as father keeps close tabs on the activities of the juvenile and prepubescent daughters or it also signifies safety concerns of the parents for their growing daughters against the evil eyes of frivolous and wanton boys. This is possibly one of the reason, the parents of today don't desire a daughter as a child. Or parents may be right in his way by not allowing adequate freedom to daughters who have broken the heart of numerous parents by indulging themselves in pre-nuptial and extra-marital activities or daughters remain unnecessary burden on their parents till they get married. So, the parents breathe a sigh of relief by transferring their burdens to their husbands.

The Indian culture and tradition is based on forbidding myth and superstition. The men have been demonical dominance over women. The former have formulated fictitious and filthy rules and rituals keeping in mind their own comfort, convenience and decadent life style at the cost of torment and exploitation of the latter. It is a sheer injustice that a widower can remarry but a widow can't, a widower can put on all kind of clothes and garments but a widow will robe only in white, a widower can relish omnivorous status but a widow will be a pure vegetarian and so on. Widower keeps on executing and fulfilling his all wishes and desires unabatedly but on widow a shackle of culture and convention is unleashed to bear bleak and barren life. Mahapatra writes a widow's woes thus:

Silent white walls of forbearance sit up
And begin to climb the stairs
Of her long inauspicious loneliness

The poet further delineates how a sex hungry man adds a woe to the worries of a widow:

Like jackals, malicious women around her,
sniffing the smell of the left over death,
feed on her scandalous intestines
through rain and summer, the spectacle or order,
through unreality and beguiling concern.

The poet is very much upset about the uncultured behavior and moral depravity of Indian women. We hardly learn good things from western culture but don't demur to discriminately imitate grey aspects of them. School, college and office going girls and women feel shame and inferiority in wearing traditional garments and clothes but they feel elated and elevated in making themselves naked and stripped to the extreme and, perhaps, this is one of the reasons of burgeoning incidents of eve teasing as such robes stir the stagnant and volcanic lust and passion of men. So, in sheer frustration, Mahapatra asks rhetorical question 'what is wrong with my country?' in the poem 'The Twenty-fifth Anniversary of a Republic':

What is wrong with my country?
the jungles have become gentle, the woman restless.
and history reposes between the college girl's breasts:
the exploits of warrior-queens, the pride pieced together
from a god's tainted armours ....
Mina, my pretty neighbor, flashes round and round the gilded stage
hiding jungles in her purse, holding on to her divorce,
and a lonely Ph.D.

The poem, 'Hunger' is one of the best examples of the circumstances which compel women to adopt the profession of prostitution. A fisherman, who is poor and penniless, doesn't hesitate to bargain the flesh of fifteen years old daughter. The poet wants to emphasize that numerous such incidents take place in our society where innocent and adolescent girls are dumped into this trade. It exposes stark reality of our contemporary society and independent India:

> I heard him say: my daughter, she's just turned fifteen.........
> feel her. I'll be back soon, your bus leaves at nine.
> The sky fell on me, and a father's exhausted wile.
> Long and lean: her years were cold as rubber.
> She opened her wormy legs wide. Felt the hunger there,
> the other one, the fish slithering, turning inside.

With the onset of evening, the common people finish their jobs but it is the time when whores come into activity. Having dressed beautifully, they flaunt on the road to woo the customers. In the poem 'Slum' Mahapatra depicts this scene:

> The familiar old whore on the road
> splits open in the sugary dusk,
> her tired breasts trailing me everywhere:
> where jackals find the rotting carcass

In his book *Dispossessed Nest* Mahapatra transcends from Oriyanness to Indianness. He crucially condemns raping and killing of innocent and naive women by the terrorists in Punjab. In the long poem, 'Bewildered Wheatfields' he writes:

> Now a man knows only two ways
> for dealing with a stray woman
> he rapes her
> and he kills her.

Even sanctum sanctorum is not devoid of heinous and atrocious activities. Every now and then the news of eve teasing flashes. We have another example of fourteen-year fisher girl, not for prostitution this time, but now being raped by petulant and perverted son of careless priest. Nevertheless, instead of bringing to book the rapist and helping to the victim, the latter is repeatedly raped by four policemen in the police station. On the one hand Mahapatra questions the viability and sanctity of temple and on the other hand condemns corrupt and promiscuous posture of police administration. The poem 'The Lost Children of America' has this note:

> In the Hanuman Temple last night
> the priest's pomaded jean-clad son
> raped squint-eyed fourteen-year fisher girl
> on the cracked stone platform behind the shrine
> and this morning
> her father found her at the police station
> assaulted over and over again by four policemen
> dripping of darkness and of scarlet death.

Mahapatra has made an ironical comment on the functioning of the government machinery and police administration. One and only cause of prostitution is poverty and this profession can be uprooted by eliminating poverty, by implementing rehabilitation programs, by providing free food and education to the children and by employing them on some jobs. In spite of taking such measures and initiatives, the government issues license to the women indulging in the flesh-trading and that further aggravates their wounds. Police nabs and persecute those prostitutes who are not in the possession of license and to get rid of police they envisage different lame excuses as a young boy does to escape evil acts from his parents. Moreover, the only source of income and livelihood for prostitutes are their flesh and skin, and with the rolling of the days, weeks, months and years, their charms and appearance get faded and they keep on losing customers. So, to hide their age and looks they go in the shelter of cosmetic illusion. Mahapatra writes in 'The Twenty-fifth Anniversary of a Republic: 1975':

> The prostitutes are younger this year:
> At the police station they're careless to give reasons
> For being what they are
> And the older women careful enough not to show
> their years.

Mahapatra has depicted both the prostitute and client in professional and commercial way. On the one hand the prostitute is in the hot haste to attend another customer because, firstly, this is only means of her sustenance. Whatever amount she gets, only a small part of that remains with her and a great chunk is devoured and extorted by the touts and the pimps. Secondly, she might have fed up with monotonous and wearisome sex, so she doesn't show curiosity and involvement with the clients. On the other hand, the client, tired and fatigued with the jobs of the day or not in good terms with his wife or miles away from home, family, wife and children to earn bread and butter, visits and pays the whore to have a kind of enlightenment and refreshment; a play and foreplay before the final play. In the poem 'The Whorehouse in a Calcutta Street', the poet describes:

> You fall back against her in the dumb light,
> trying to learn something more about women—
> while she does what she thinks proper to please
> you,
> the sweet, the little things, the imagined;
> until the statute of the man within
> you've believed in throughout the years
> comes back to you, a disobeying toy—
> and the walls you wanted to pull down
> mirror only of things mortal, and passing by;

> like a girl holding on to your wide wilderness;
> as though it were real, as though the renewing voice
> tore the membrane of your half-woken mind
> when, like a door, her words close behind:
> "Hurry, will you? Let me go."
> and her lonely breath thrashed against your kind.

In the poem 'Absence', we have another instance of communication but indirect one between the client and the whore where the former, though with guilty conscience, pledges to exploit and consummate the flesh of the latter by optimal degree:

> When the windows shut down on your thighs
> my hands quiver with the glances of my thousand eyes
> as your long eyes touch my paid-out pain
> and I revenge the presence from your presence.

Mahapatra's poetry deftly demonstrates the weal and woes of women. It incorporates various vice and virtues associated with them. He comes out with a solution for the pain and predicament they are confronted with. He makes use of the legend of ogress Putna for this very purpose. Afraid of prophecy of being killed by the God Krishna, the mammoth monster Kansa sends the ogress Putna to assassinate the incarnated child Krishna. As illusive she was, she metamorphosed herself into a beautiful and motherly figure. She smeared venom on her breasts and offered milk to the child. The child, Krishana sucked and soaked her up to death. If we go by the myth and the scripture, ogress Putna registered 'Moksha' or salvation by receiving death at the hands of the god Krishna because she offers two things simultaneously: evil and good; hemlock and nectar; venom and milk; for the former she is penalized death and for playing the role of mother, she is awarded 'Moksha'.

The poet wants to substantiate that as Putna achieved salvation by virtue of her own acts, the women can also keep their sufferings at bay only by their own deeds i.e. their redemption solely subsists on their womanhood. Otherwise they were, they are and they will be bearing the brunt of man-made manacle. As a poet, he tries to break the shackles that have been tied around the women restricting their movements by the orthodox patriarchal society.

References

1. Das, Bijay Kumar. *The Poetry of Jayanta Mahapatra*: New Delhi: Atlantic, 2001, p. 56.
2. Sarangi, Jaydeep and Jha, Gauri Shankar. *The Indian Imagination of Jayanta Mahapatra.* New Delhi: Sarup and Sons, 2006, p. 89.
3. Das, Bijay Kumar. *Twentieth century literary criticism*. New Delhi: Atlantic, 2001, p.102.
4. Mahapatra, Jayanta. *Poems and Other Stories*. Hyderabad: Disha Books, 1997.
5. Moi,Toril, ed. *French Feminist Thought: A Reader*. NewYork, Oxford: Basil Blackwell, 1987, p. 122.
6. Source: http:/WWW.geocities.com/bororissa/mamata.html.
7. Showalter, Elaine, ed. *The New Feminist criticism: Essays on Women, Literature, and Theory*. New York: Pantheon Books, 1985, p. 363.

11

Niranjan Mohanty's Poetry: A Journey to the Soul of India

Ashok Kumar

Prof. Niranjan Mohanty (1953-2008) has lived last part of his life at Visva-Bharati, Santiniketan—an accommodation of Rabindranath Tagore. He has captivated, enthralled, and embellished the literary world with his prolific and vibrant writings. He is a man of multi-faceted literary genius, a luminous star shining brightly and enjoys a conspicuous and unassailable place in Indo-Anglian literature. He is a candid assessor of Indian Literature in English, a fanatical teacher and an established rhymester too. Striding the literary world as a colossus, Mohanty has played a pivotal role in the acceleration and mellowness of Indian Literature in English. He was only and the eldest son to his parents and had one younger sister too. Concerning his nature he explores: "I am very simple; cool-minded having enough patience, well understanding & compromising, optimistic & hard working, affectionate & God-fearing person."[1]

Mohanty was enthused and touched by the great English masterminds. That possibly, tangentially rather, forced him towards reading more English poets. When he felt that he is self-assured in English he·instigated writing in English. By this time, he didn't come across any of Indian poets. Subsequent to Intermediate in Science, he was fascinated to the Romantics and the Modern poets. He was drawn to the beauty of language, the felicity of expression in English. In the meantime he was influenced by T.S. Eliot, W.B. Yeats, Walt Whitman and Wallace Stevens etc. Concerning his advancement in English literature he says:

> "Obviously, my training in English Literature helped me a great deal to become a poet in English. For my training in English literature I was fortunate enough to read the great poets of the West. They continue to attract me since my college days. I can never ignore the influence of Shelley, Keats, Donne, Shakespeare, Eliot and Yeats when I was first introduced to them."[2]

Some other great poets like John Keats and John Donne became his favourite in a later phase. He likes the verses of Ramakanta Rath, Sitakanta Mahapatra, Hira Prasad Paricha and Bipin Nayek too. But, he is always reminded of another significant voice in Oriya poetry like Bibek Jena, who is no more. In the formative stage of Mohanty's creative career he was deeply influenced by Pablo Neruda too. The intensity in the lines of their poems hypnotized him. The seer magic of words and the rhythmical beauty, they created in their poems, were the sources of his great inspiration. Even if Mohanty's first language is Oriya and he has written a number of verses in Oriya too, published in *Jhankar and Asanta Kali*. He also enumerated his Oriya poems for All India Radio, Berhampur and Cuttack.

Prof. Mohanty has published six volumes of poems (*Silence the Words, On Touching You and Other Poems, Life Lines, Prayers to Lord Jagannath, Oh This Bloody Game!* and *Krishna*). His verses have emerged in magazines and journals in India, U.K., U.S.A., and Canada. He has been awarded with Honorary Writing Fellow at the International

Writing Program, The University of Iowa, Iowa City, U.S.A. in 1994. Prof. Mohanty has translated a lot of literary works from Oriya and Bengali into English and from Bengali into Oriya. Sahitya Akademi, New Delhi has published *Nirjhar* (2006), a volume of sixty poems of Jibanananda Das in Oriya translation. His verses as well have been translated into Hindi, Spanish, Portuguese and Urdu. Inward-looking, and at the same time, deeply entrenched in intellectual and interpersonal realities, his poems speak to us with frank generosity and the mystery of life coming through the linguistic mélange of his creative utterance. His willing leap into the pool of memories creates a sense of presence through the metaphors of absence. The haunting presence of the metaphor of death invests his poems with a sense of mystery, a sense that is unverifiable, and non-negotiable by reason or intellect. An absence continues to haunt the poet since childhood. The fleeting nature of time always chants a sweeping sense of absence. He speaks for the mystery of love, the mystical element embodied in the man-woman relationship. His poetry reveals and celebrates "blue whispers of hearts, immaculate," the innocence ingrained in sense of mortality, in the immaculate sense of things passed by.[3] Regarding the themes of his verses he further says:

> "There are no strong or weak themes. To me, life itself is the central theme in my poetry. The mortality we live in and breathe in and whatever shapes or moulds punctuate—time, death, absences, loneliness, the inner struggle and the burdens of uncountable dreams constitute the themes of my poetry. Like Neruda, I can say, "I am the professor of life and a very vague student of death." To write poetry in any language, for that matter, the poet has to love life in its multiple voices and forms. This way of comprehending life into the fold of one's creative vision enables one to discover order out of disorder; meaning amidst apparent

> meaninglessness. ..... A poet cannot do that without developing a relationship with life itself. I believe, this is another form of *bhakti* that attracts the poets—the *bhakti* that refines the experience and intensifies the expression."[4]

Mohanty's poetry is rich in symbols and imagery, because he has a creative energy and is 'a poet who knows that poetry alone could make others share his central experience.' A variety of significant symbols he has used in his poetry are 'tiger', 'house', 'family', 'journey' and 'absence'. This may be because of the loss of his near and dear ones: his brother (1958), sister (1958), grandmother (1964) and his father (1994). Absence is inevitable in life and one can never recover from it. The conception of absence makes the presence evocative. He makes his presence felt through absences. About the use of symbols and imagery he further says:

> "Possibly, the important symbols in my poetry are 'tiger', 'house', 'family', 'journey' and 'absence'. Every tiger poem uses 'tiger' differently. Tiger is synonymous with destruction. It also stands for life force. 'Tiger' in my poems can be read as hunger, sexuality, death and silence—a meaningful silence. Tiger, an animal when turned into symbol, records the graph of my experiences—the multifaceted dilemma of existence, leading to the certitude of silence. 'Home' and 'Family' occupy a large space in my poetry because of their eternal and abiding capacities for love, security, and peace. 'Journey' remains a significant motif in my poems. The journey through words takes me to every corner of life and allows me to understand the secret recesses of my sense of modality......The knowledge of absence makes the presence meaningful. I make my presence felt through absences."[5]

Mohanty's notoriety in Indian English poetry rests on

his two protracted poems, *Prayers to Lord Jagannath,* dealing with metaphysical myths and legends of Lord Jagannath and *Krishna,* which is about the *bhakti* tradition in Indian religious space in relation with the myth of Krishna. His poetry demonstrates a far-reaching high degree of divine tolerance and happiness ensuing from a practice of marvellous grace. He has initiated his writing profession as early as 1977, with his foremost compilation of poems *Silencing the Words* (1977), and since then he has published five more collections: *Oh This Bloody Game* (1980), *Prayers to Lord Jagannath* (1994), *On Touching You and Other Poems* (1999), *Life Lines* (1999), and *Krishna: A Long Poem* (2003). In his *Oh This Bloody Game*—the second volume of poems—he has made an effort to comprehend himself, his life and art and reveals intensely the human in him with apprehension for the down-trodden, prostitutes, victims of flood and drought, and so on. Mohanty has tried to imitate quite meditativeness, slightly touched with sorrow and nostalgia, the ubiquitous religious and cultural ambience of Orissa, which gives its distinctive quality to his verse. Even his method of expression, and the use of imagery and phrasing replace conventional poetic argument, so that meaning is always hinted at but not directly conveyed nor fully grasped. All these features are most clearly apparent in his, *Prayers to Lord Jagannath.*[6] In his poetry he exposes to a lot of humanity and his soul survives in spite of great difficulties for a fruitful survival. His kinship with the Oriyan culture and traditions, and his enriched productive perception with Lord Jagannath, and his responsiveness for various changes taking place in society day by day, he himself as a poet continues to accomplish sensation in all his forthcoming assortment of poetry.

Mohanty has conducted research amongst primeval incidents and exposes himself in anticipation of the lost world, anguish, throbbing annoyance and sense of irrelevances. His works—lyrical and contemplative—look to sensationalize the self rather than to discover a number of greater truth or actuality. We receive an inspiration of the paradox of Infinite Power and Infinite Tenderness also, and for the devotee this gives genuine contentment. His first long poem, *Prayers to Lord Jagannath,* is paradigm of his experiments with meditation, exploration, devotion, and celebration of humanity and divinity simultaneously.

His verses are grand since his poetry replicates an era. He brings out verve and an assortment of types of men and approach in their accurate colours. His poetry makes a dialogue between the present and the past with an eye to future. His triumph, excellence and dexterity are revealed in his socio-human analysis which redeems, sanctifies and ennobles. As a poet of high calibre, talking to Lord Jagannath so intimately that he can seed, love, abhor, reduce and esteem him, though for the moment, philosophy appears conceited the devise of the whole story. He further explores, "Sometimes....I'm not clear in what I write/I fail to grasp the meaning of what I chisel." (Prayers to Lord Jagannath) In his verses, Mohanty has specified a very demanding pose of the Lord Jagannath, whose gargantuan arms connote His warmth for the entire cosmos, never vacillating or disappointing the underprivileged or passionate disciple. In His territory, nobody is invulnerable and confers harmony to the fussy heart and cools down one's everyday afflictions. He is the culmination of man's quest for joy, love and peace. He reveals himself as a poet of reliance, without being critical, or building any daring proclamation. Even then, he confronts the presiding divinity of Orissa as an entity of flesh and blood who is not devoid of human failings he puts question mark on every bustle performed by the Lord Jagannath that to the human judgment is not foolproof:

> Whose turn is it now to sleep?
> Whose turn is it to weep? Whose turn is it?
> To murmur goodbye, to become silence?
>
> (Prayers to Lord Jagannath)

Mohanty surprises us occasionally with an unusual image or a lapidary phrase: "the heart.... /restless like the sea". (Naik and Narayan 182) But otherwise he is prone to lapsing into solecisms: "procession of cavalries" and "Lord of tendrils... tambourine....Telegrams", (Lord Jagannath must be connected with the post office, because alliteration demands it). (183) His *Krishna: A Long Poem* is an effort to reveal the Divine Game and devotion to the Lord Krishna. This is also a means of self-searching, self-understanding, or knowing intellectual powers more closely. Here Mohanty's cogitate is embedded in the vigilantly and dexterously sophisticated dedication towards the antique ethnicity and splendid times of yore. He has applied the mechanism— kind of restricted access to himself—with a shrewdness of detection, pledge, and collapse. He writes in 'Krishna: A Long Poem':

> I searched you here, there
> And almost everywhere.
> Nowhere I found you.
> Woe-struck, I sculptured my loneliness
> On the sleek back of darkness.
> A voice from the dark told me
> To look within. As I looked
> Within myself, I found you there, sleeping
> Like the trail of dreams
> Of my own making.

He has made an attempt to settle the reliability of his own delicate self concerning the outline of communal cohesion, decent hallucination, and metaphysical puzzles that the myths and legends of the Lord Jagannath and Krishna customarily make available to show one a way through the dimness of a hectic way of life.

The poet's commitment is for the *Saguna* stream of poetry—for the most part interrelated to the *Vaishnava* poets—who had two dissimilar, although associated schools: *Krishna Bhakti* and *Rama Bhakti*. Together Krishna and Rama are two incarnations of Vishnu and therefore there need not be any serious conflict. *Krishna bhakti* is the vital spring of inspiration for him. In this poem Mohanty wishes to delineate to the masses that both Radha and Krishna, physically and piously are deficient without each other yet in prayers, he further eulogizes (in Krishna: A Long Poem),

> Can we contrast a silence, when
> I'm all fires and you, all ashes?

Mohanty is a quite devoted worshipper of Krishna, who has composed quite a lot of poems, which are mostly lyrical. He uses the metaphor of 'prayers' and love to refurbish the troubled equilibrium, both superficially and inside. His insurgent psyche continues to be overwhelmed by "the storm of irrelevance/blowing past the fence/of my benign bones chanting ever/the songs of my morality," to quote from one of his earlier poems, 'A Winter Evening.'[7] He further divulges Krishna engrossed in Radha, in respect of the unification of husband and wife in the creative pair. His poignant, demonstrative and conjugal advice coursing through the mind-body complex disseminate outwards to be converted into love or bliss of devotion, which is adulation. Krishna adores Radha exposing the divine energy in human as the sexual advice. The revelation of God as love/devotee adds a reminder of theology, which may also be cherished in requisites of the affection of Vaishnavism. His symphony as a full time devotee of Krishna in the poems of love is par excellence. His adulation for Krishna would move anybody, who is benevolent, and his verses are, in fact, redolent to those who ascertain their definitive legitimacy in adores.

Mohanty portrays the phases of Radha's adoration for Krishna in an ingenious demeanour. His poem, 'Krishna: A Long Poem' brings out the dynamism of Radha's love after she has capitulated to the fascination of Krishna:

I'm the Gardner of her dreams.
I'm the dream of her sleep.
I'm the gist of her silence and song.

In his doggerel, Mohanty comes into view to have established the primordial Hindu observation that the allure of connubial care in human being is natural. He more seems to blend this heavenly power within, and tries to make the individual and humanity in close proximity by focusing on a society with strong sexual association. As a consequence, his poetry endows with a description of the emotional sumptuousness and divine sparkle of the devotional writings and eulogizes the objective brilliance of his adored and articulates the powerful yearning for substantial amalgamation with her lacking of being erotic, and he sees no shrewdness in conceiving adoration as "abstract, distant, or dizzy", to a certain extent affection exudes inviolability. At this assessment Mohanty says,

> Krishna unhesitating, nobly, humbly, honesty, goes on narrating, sculpting his love for Radha. The startling fusion of the mythic, the divine and the human in these two archetypal personalities subverts, dissipates and dissolves the archetypes and creates a space for the human, the mortal. Because of the gravitational force of the element of mystery attached to the divine, the poem subverts the divine and celebrates what is human through love as the central metaphor.[8]

Mohanty's latest tiger poems remind us of "T.S Eliot for the postmodern application of symbols; inter-textuality and concrete metaphors that describe the fuzzy zones of modern life."[9] Mohanty's poems record and celebrate 'blue whispers of hearts, immaculate.' He writes:

The flavour of rice
Boiling on an earthen- pot
under the thatched roof
Sheltering voices.

He has left no stone unturned in unearthing and exploring the miscellaneous facets of life. In doing so, despite a deep wretchedness embedded in the poems, Mohanty sings the theme-song of life, unpretentiously celebrating the rhythms of life. Neither through denunciation nor through protestation, but through a willing acceptance of life as meaningful, he has matured as a poet, with a distinct poetic vision, a distinct poetic utterance, and an immaculate sense of belonging to his own country, culture and tradition.[18] Mohanty's new volume of poems, *Tiger and Other Poems (2008)* evinces a discernible exodus. Tiger, that has occupied his thought-process since the 1980s, assumes in the poems of this volume, a dimension that only the symbolic mode can comprehend and illustrate.

Hence, triumph and dexterity achieved by him is a perfect blending of feeling, theme, technique, art and mysticism. His expressions are not rigid, complex and pedantic and they never impair the flow and receptivity of the readers. They, on the other hand, enhance the beauty and the theme of the poem and turn the poem into an organic whole. In consequence, it is prevalent, as devotion is an integral part of every creed and India is known for its receptivity to all religions and faiths. So whatever may be the source of inspiration for the various poems of devotion, as literary pieces, Prof. Mohanty's poetry has incredibly ample elation.

Prof. Niranjan Mohanty is one such name who has raised plenteous issues associated to man and existing civilization all the way through his poetry. It is interesting to note here that genuine poetry is born out of a delicate balance between a perfect theme which is beyond caste, class and creed and a conscious mastery of words and phrases mastered in such a way that the outer structure, the style and the technique are enough to suggest the sense. This is exactly what we find in the poetry of Mohanty as he chooses his phrases and dictions with care and handle them with balance. Nevertheless, on July 28, 2008 his sudden demise at 55 has stunned the literary world and his unfortunate departure is undoubtedly an irretrievable loss to Indian Poetry in English.

References

1. http://immatri.rediff.com/scripts/findmore.php?userid=1937943.
2. An interview with Niranjan Mohanty by Jaydeep Sarangi, http://christopherrollason.spaces.live.com/blog/cns!459178C2F5215F32!53.entry.
3. *Ibid.*
4. *Ibid.*
5. *Ibid.*
6. Naik, M.K. & Shyamla A. Narayan, *Indian English Literature–(1980-2000) A Critical Survey,* New Delhi: Pencraft International, 2001, p. 182.
7. Mohanty, Niranjan *Oh This Bloody Game.* Berhampur: Poetry Publications, 1988, p. 15.
8. Datta, Vandna "Meet the Author: An Interview with Niranjan Mohanty," *Research,* Vol. 04, No. 02 (Autumn-2004), p. 69.
9. http://www.museindia.com/showcurrent10.asp?id =1060.
10. https://www.vedamsbooks.com/no58374.htm

Works Cited

Mohanty, Niranjan. *Prayers to Lord Jagannath.* New Delhi: Indus, 1994.

____________ . *Tiger and Other Poems.* New Delhi: Sarup and Sons, 2008.

____________ . *Krishna: A Long Poem.* Bhubaneswar: Avanti, 2003.

Amga, H.L. *Indo-English Poetry.* Jaipur: Surabhi, 2000.

Prasad, A. N. *Studies in Indian Poetry in English.* New Delhi: Sarup & Sons, 2003.

Prasad, A. N. & Sarkar, Brithika (eds.) *Critical Response to Indian Poetry in English.* New Delhi: Sarup & Sons, 2008.

Mishra, Binod. *Festival of Fire.* Delhi: Adhyayan Publishers, 2010.

Dutta A. (ed.) *Encyclopedia of Indian Literature* (EIL) Vols I, II, & III, New Delhi: Sahitya Academi, 1989.

Sharma, Krishna. *Bhakti Movement: A New Perspective,* Delhi: Munshiram Manoharlal, 1987.

Mukherji, Sujit. *Towards A Literary History of India,* Shimla: IIAS, 1975.

Iyengar K. R. Srinivasa, (ed.) *Indian Literature Since Independence.* New Delhi: Sahitya Akademi, 1973.

Verma, M.R. *Reflections on Indian English Literature.* New Delhi: Atlantic, 2002.

Sethuraman V.S., (ed.), *Indian Aesthetics: An Introduction.* Madras: Macmillan, 1992.

12

Gender Sensitivity and Indian English Women's Poetry

Bhavesh Chandra Pandey

Gender is a cultural construct and the concepts of masculinity and femininity have been built up in the course of evolution. Separate codes were built around masculinity and femininity leading gradually to widely different roles and expectations. The biological differences in respect of sex turned into inequality in respect of gender. So, women started to be treated not only different from man but also inferior. Consequently, a social structure emerged in which man had the upper hand. The role of women in the society was determined less by biology than by socially evolved definitions of gender. In this context Simone de Beauvoir's remark assumes great significance as she said that one is not born woman, one becomes one. It signifies that biology merely produces the girl child. It is the sociology that shapes the identity of woman. This identity imposed on her by culture governs her role.

Literature is an important social attribute and an integral part of culture. It reflects the society and also shapes it. The social roles and codes attributed to women are reflected in it. The socially ascribed morality is also constructed by literature. In it we can see the reflection of history, ethics, anthropology and sociology. The cultural connotations of gender are also reflected in it. It is also sometimes a colonizing agent as it sometimes propagates the dogma of slavery by upholding the patriarchal moral superstructure.

With the emergence of the patriarchal social structure the very notion of masculinity became important. Matriarchy as a system has failed. In patriarchy women are treated as mentally and physically 'frail', intellectually 'inferior' and spiritually unblessed. They are held responsible for the fall of man. This responsibility has made her liable to the custody of man. The Bible declares- "Thy desire shall be to thy husband and he shall rule over thee". This divine declaration seems to have given man the moral authority over women as St. Paul says: "For the man is not for woman, but women for the man". Therefore women are supposed to be under male's control and to serve and satisfy them. The overall image of women is that of 'colonized', marginalized, deprived, dependant, exploited, and suppressed. They are kept under moral sanctions and are forced to bear the moral stigma. Men enjoy the status of guardians and hold the authority to define their codes of conduct. Women have been treated as subjugated and their subjection is morally sanctioned by religion and philosophy.

The Indian English women poets grew up in a culture that has given diverse representation to women. On the one hand they have been treated as symbol of power, devotion, emotion, service, sacrifice, beauty, kindness etc. On the other hand they have been treated as weak, submissive, and irrational. They are expected to be under veil, preserve their chastity, please their partners, serve their family and bear moral sanctions. They are conditioned for the voluntary acceptance of subjugation as their religious duty. They are to treat men as their 'protectors' and 'maintainers'. The society expects them to accept the phallocentric, patriarchal superstructure and to fit in the male-dominated moral system.

They are sensitive to the issues concerning women in the culture they belong and seem to respond to their crises in a feministic fashion. In them we can notice an honest yearning for a comfortable room in the male-dominated social frame. We can find sometimes a genuine cry for love and sometimes a revolt against the imposition of codes. They express at times a mild complaint and at times an angry protest against the male mentality. They show an acute sensitivity to gender issues similar to that sown in the poems of Anne Sexton, Judith Wright and Sylvia Plath.

Indian English women poets in the post-Independence era have shown their sensitivity to the gender issues in a more tangible manner. The poetry of Kamala Das, Gauri Deshpande, Mamata Kalia, Eunice D'Souza, and Lakshami Kannan displays feminine sensitivity quite unequivocally.

Kamala Das is undoubtedly the most powerful spokesperson of women issues. "Kamala Das's is a fiercely feminine sensibility that dares without inhibitions to articulate the hurts it has received in an insensitive largely man-made world." (Iyengar 680) She has tried to establish her reputation as the 'femme fatale' of Indo -Anglian poetry. Her confessional poetry is a sustained exercise in the promiscuous self-expose and an expression of self-exhibition and deadening sex and sensuality. She honestly expresses her hurt, disillusion and cynicism.

In her poem 'An introduction', she points out to the moral conditioning imposed on women by the society. She says that a girl child is continually conditioned to accept her codes and fit in the moral frame. The males act as the categorizers as they have the authority to shape and identify women. She writes:

> Dress in saris, be girl,
> Be wife, they said. Be embroiderer, be cook,
> Be a quarreller with servants. Fit in. oh,
> Belong, cried the categorizers. (33-36)

By asking to accept the dress and professional stereotypes the society prepares them to belong to the feminine set up. Men create a value system in which women feel suppressed and they become 'dwarf'. Kamala Das has constantly revolted against this imposition. She writes in the poem 'The Old Playhouse':

> ....Cowering
> Beneath your monstrous ego I ate the magic loaf and
> Became a dwarf. I lost my will and reason, to all your
> Questions I mumbled incoherent replies. (14-17)

Kamla Das presents a feminine approach to husband-wife relationship. She tells how her personality was ignored and how she received male lessons. She could not recognize herself in the company of man. She writes:

> ...I came to you but to learn
> What I was, and by learning to learn to grow, but every
> Lesson you gave was about yourself. (6-8)

This rigorous training and conditioning made her lose her 'will and reason'. The sensitivity of Das extends not only to the male and the female but also to the eunuchs. She expresses their sense of helplessness in the poem 'The Dance of the Eunuchs'. The eunuchs have to bear a sorry fate as they are 'other' both to man and woman. Kamala Das expresses a sense of compassion for them. She writes thus:

> Some beat their drums; others beat their sorry breasts
> And wailed, and writhed in vacant ecstasy. They
> Were thin in limbs and dry; like half-burnt logs from

Funeral pyres, a drought and a rottenness
Were each of them. (12-16)

Kamala Das talks with an 'uninhibited frankness' about sex. But her persona is not the nymphomaniac. She is simply 'every woman who seeks love' expressing the 'endless female hungers'. In her 'heart of hearts' she is 'the eternal Eve proudly celebrating her essential femininity'. (Naik 209) Her favourite theme has been sex and body's wisdom. The total impression of poetry is one of bold ruthless honesty, tearing passionately at conventional attitudes to reveal the quintessential woman within. Gauri Deshpande questions the utility of men in discussing genuine concerns of women.

There is a clear sense of rejection of men as partner in dealing with crisis in life. Women can have a better understanding of the problems of women. Mamata Kalia is even bolder in her pronouncement of revolt against the authority of men. In her poem 'A Tribute to Papa' she expresses her will to disown her father. She writes:

These days I am seriously thinking of
Disowning you Papa...
Everything about you clashes with nearly
Everything about me.

Eunice de Souza is another Indian 'confessional' poet. She also works for her identity. She breaks the fetters of conventionality and propriety itself. She writes:

Forgive me, mother
In dreams, I hack you.

The overall response of women poets has been that of reaction and revolt against the existing value system which has historically served predominantly male interest. It has attempted to be an antidote to the existing value-system. However, the tone and orientation of women

'Inglish' poetry needs to undergo a change. There appears to be a focus on cultural androgyny and a comfortable co-existence between man and woman rather than a mudslinging on men. Most women poets are occupied with the question of 'identity' and seem to be ignorant of some other more serious threats to the existence of women. Nevertheless, they have invented the appropriate idiom for striking at the root of the patriarchal system. The frankness and uninhibited, unambiguous force of expression augurs well for a promising future. The poetry is born out of the lived experience and therefore it is transparent, direct, unequivocal and forceful. The poets show the guts to reject taboos and stigma and express freely the religion of blood. They sincerely yearn for the realization of womanhood.

Works Cited

Aurobindo, Sri. *The Human Cycle*. Pondicherry: Aurobindo Ashram, 1992.

Gokak, V.K., ed. *The Golden Treasury of Indo-Anglian Poetry*. New Delhi: Sahitya Academy, 2006.

Iyengar, K. R. Srinivas. *Indian Writing in English*. New Delhi: Sterling Publishers, 2001.

Naik, M. K. *A History of Indian English Literature*. New Delhi: Sahitya Academy, 1995.

Panikkar, K. M., ed. *Modern Indian Poetry in English*. New Delhi: Sahitya Academy, 2006.

Peeradina, S., ed. *Contemporary Indian Poetry in English*. New Delhi: Macmillan, [illegible]

13

'Humour' as a Tool of Poetic Communication: A Comparative Study of Maha Nand Sharma and I.K. Sharma.

Ram Kulesh Thakur and *R. K. Singh*

"The highest form of intelligence is creativity, and the highest form of creativity is humour."[1] Almost every major figure in the history of philosophy has proposed a theory for humour, but even after 2500 years of discussion there has been little consensus about what constitutes humour. Great philosophers such as Aristotle, Plato, Immanuel Kant, Kierkegaard, Thomas Hobbes, Sigmund Freud, Herbert Spencer, and a [illegible]ber of thinkers have given their opinion on 'humour,' and [illegible]efore the concept has been one of the most radically [illegible] concepts. [2]

The present paper [illegible]ng
understanding on 'humour[illegible] into account the general
age. In the present time, 'hu[illegible]oped in the contemporary
tendency of particular images, [illegible] is believed to be the
provoke laughter and amusement. [illegible]s, or situations to
'amusement' as the keywords in the [illegible]d 'laughter' and
In fact, laughter and amusement are ge[illegible]on provided.
[illegible]nly when

one comes across something unexpected; something that breaks the rules, or one's expectation; something that is incongruous. We may find here an echo of Aristotle's *Rhetoric,* where it is stated that the best way to get an audience to laugh is to set up an expectation and deliver something "that gives a twist." [4] In the *Critique of Judgement,* Immanuel Kant gives a clearer statement on the role of incongruity in humour: "In everything that is to excite a lively laugh there must be something absurd (in which the understanding, therefore, can find no satisfaction). Laughter is an affection arising from the sudden transformation of a strained expectation into nothing." [5] Alastair Clarke, another renowned theorist, also expresses a similar idea and explains that humour occurs when the brain recognises a pattern that surprises it, and that recognition of this sort is rewarded with the experience of the humourous response, an element of which is broadcast as laughter.[6]

When we approach Sanskrit Poetics, we find a similar discussion in the *Rasa Theory*. 'Rasa' literally means taste or savour, and it signifies the peculiar experience that poetry affords to a reader. It is the sympathetic flow of emotions in the heart of the spectator or the reader after the depiction of an image, situation, or story in the literary text. The depiction of any such thing in poetry is through words having an emotive significance and the emotions evoked through their medium are enjoyed actively by the reader; the evoked emotion being the 'rasa.' Of the eight major 'rasas' classified, the 'hasya rasa' is responsible for evoking laughter and amusement in the reader or audience.[7]

In the light of the above discussion, a few poems of I. K. Sharma and Maha Nand Sharma have been analysed to study the creation and use of humour by them for the purpose of poetic communication.

I. K. Sharma, with his six collections of poetry, has established himself as a social and political realist. Although most of his poems concerned with society, politics, and economy of the country, are rich in the use of irony and satire as tools of communication, the poems dealing with the minor themes use humour to a good extent.

The first poem taken for analysis is 'Mosquito' from the collection *My Lady, Broom and Other Poems* (2004).[8]

> The boss of the night
> pays stinging respects
> to my toes before feasting
> on other limbs.
> ....
> ....
> The kid of Hell mocks
> at every item of creation
> that spends hours in a bunk:
> a babe, a mother, or a hunk.

In the first stanza of the poem, the poet addresses mosquito as 'the boss of the night,' and the use of the word 'boss' for a tiny insect creates humour. The use of the phrase 'pays stinging respects' in the second line followed by 'to my toes ...'adds to the humour taking into account the Indian cultural considerations. In Indian tradition, touching one's feet is a way to show one's respect for the other person, especially an elder. The poet develops a similar context in the stanza where a mosquito is depicted paying his respect to the poet. The poet adds to the humour by using the witty remark 'stinging respects,' where 'stinging' is a negative modifier used for modifying a positive entity 'respect.'

In the next stanza, the poet compares the movement of a mosquito with that of a bomber plane, and the comparison itself evokes humour, as a mosquito is a very small creature in comparison to a plane. The poet, in a humorous tone, describes how a mosquito soars, dives, and lands on his ear or nose.

In the third stanza of the poem, the poet uses the word

'singing' for the humming sound produced by a mosquito. The poet deliberately uses the word 'singing' in the stanza to rhyme it with 'stinging,' and the rhyme between a negative quality 'stinging' and the positive quality 'singing' creates humour in the given context. The poet uses the phrase 'cauldron of witches' for the bodily cavity of human being, and it displays wit along with humour.

The use of 'I' repetitively for four times in short phrases, in the first line of the fourth stanza, creates a humorous tone in the poem. The phrasal construction in the beginning of the stanza displays equivalence with the movement of a mosquito, and the reader gets an impression that the speaker is continuously being bit by the mosquito. The use of punctuation marks to create adequate pauses between the short phrases gives a realistic impression of the narration to the reader. The poet's effort to imprison the mosquito, and in the process gaining a new thrust and impetus is humorous.

In the sixth stanza of the poem, the poet unveils a very minute observation on his part. It is observed that the mosquitoes have a tendency of sitting at the same spot of the body from where they have been chased away, which may be because they have prepared that part of the skin ready for their sucking activity, and such an idea evokes humour. The rhyming between the last two lines of the stanza imparts a humorous tone to the poem. The repetition of the 'R' sound, a number of times, in the last two lines suggests that the speaker is in real pain.

In the last stanza of the poem, the speaker addresses the mosquito as 'The kid of Hell', and this evokes humour as the speaker was using good and positive phraseology for the mosquito in the beginning. The shift of emotion from 'admiration' to 'hatred' (for the mosquito) as the narration proceeds is humorous. The speaker also depicts that a mosquito mocks at all such creatures, which waste their several hours in sleeping. The use of the rhyming words 'bunk' and 'hunk' in the last two lines of the poem also creates humour as it suggests that even a hunk (adult human being) likes to spend his time in a bunk (not a place for human being).

The next poem taken for analysis is 'The Guestorm (II)' from the collection *The Shifting Sand-Dunes* (1976).[9] The title of the poem 'Guestorm' is a typical coinage by the poet himself, as he could not find any recognised equivalent word to express his conception of a guest. The title itself is very suggestive as it is coined by blending two English words 'Guest' and 'Storm'; guest followed by storm. The title suggests a multiple of meaning such as: guest comes like a storm (without any prior notice or information); guest is more often destructive in nature (as a storm); guest creates disturbances and unsettles the normal life; and the departure of a guest is never fixed as in the case of a storm. The title also suggests that the quantity of guests cannot be restricted or checked, as the intensity of a storm is beyond bounds. Thus, we find an undertone of humour in the selection of the title itself.

The whole poem is composed in the style of a conversation, and the first stanza straightaway exposes the readers to the conversation between two brother-in-laws:

> Brother, you are a man of wide contacts
> can fix up your nephew somewhere,
> anywhere you like—
> you are the best judge of the situation.
> I shall send him on to you soon—
> very soon. He will be under your eyes,
> for, out of sight, out of mind.
> He wants service. I can't give him.
> You can. You try. I shall send him soon.
> Staying here six months without service
> will not be a disadvantage.
> ....
> ....
> Yes, I shall send the money through MO
> as I get the news of his admission.

Taking into account the Indian cultural considerations, the relationship between brother-in-laws is always congenial. They crack jokes upon each other and enjoy each other's company, although they get irritated sometimes. Thus, we may observe that the setting of the poem itself evokes humour. The other remarkable humorous aspect of the poem is that there is only one person (guest) speaking throughout the poem, and the other is a meek silent listener. The tone of the poem further adds to the humour by suggesting that the speaker does not give his listener any chance to speak, or even express his consent or disagreement, in regard to the questions or opinion posed by him. The speaker in the poem is a guest to his brother-in-law's house, and has stormed there with a well set plan and a number of requests to be obliged with. The speech of the speaker clearly reveals that he intends to send most of his family members to the host's house in near future, and has a very strong undeniable pretext for each of them.

The speaker talks of sending one of his sons to his brother-in-law with a request of getting him placed somewhere. The poet uses 'enjambment' as a device to evoke humour in the third line of the stanza. Enjambment is used as a subtle mean of giving a reader more freedom to interpret the meaning of the given line and draw his own conclusion in relation to the given context. Here, the technique evokes humour as a reader gets to know the real intention of the speaker in the given context, and that is to get his son placed anywhere and anyhow. The repetition of the word 'soon' thrice shows the urgency on the part of the guest, and it again evokes humour. The absence of any consent on the part of the host shows his reluctance, but the insistence on the part of the speaker makes him helpless, and this helplessness adds to the humour in the given context. The use of long gaps between the full stops and the first word of the next sentence in the eighth and ninth line of the stanza provides a longer halt than a full stop, and thus, changes the tone of the poem. This change in tone of the poem gives a realistic touch to the speech and thus adds to the humour. The last two lines of the stanza take the humour to a new height as it manifests that the guest is only thinking of his advantage, and not of the host. The staying of his son for six months at the host's house would, under no circumstance, be a disadvantage to him, but on the part of the host, it would not be the same.

In the next stanza of the poem, the guest gives an account of his daughters' last year visit to the host's house. The speaker bestows praises on the host, on behalf of his daughters, to please him. The stanza reveals that the visit made by the speaker is not the beginning, but a continuation to the chain of visits made by his family members to his brother-in-law's house. The use of a native word 'bhabhi' twice, which is disyllabic and trochaic, changes the tone of the stanza as most of the words of the stanza are monosyllabic in nature, also yields to humour.

In the next stanza, the guest informs his brother-in-law that Kamal (probably his younger brother, son, or a near relative) is neither healthy nor doing well in his studies these days. The doctors and teachers have advised to change his place and company respectively, and so he is thinking of sending him here, at the host's house.

The succeeding stanza is a sort of justification, which he provides to convince his brother-in-law, for his decision of sending Kamal to this place. The reason, which he states as a justification, is that Kamal would get a good academic atmosphere in the company of the host and his children. The fourth line of the stanza, "HE does not bother about children at all" is a digression from the main dialogue as 'HE' is used for God. This sort of a digression amidst the main dialogue helps the purpose of evoking humour. Resuming the main dialogue, the visitor states that Kamal would even be able to make use of the personal collection of books, which the host has, without paying any costs for it. The eighth line, "freely available to him," displays the money-minded attitude of the speaker, which evokes humour in the given context. In the last four lines of the stanza, the speaker guarantees the expected improvement in Kamal, to stress upon his insistence on the host and get his consent in the regard.

In the first two lines of the fifth stanza, the visitor showers praises on the host to take him into confidence. The guest praises the host for bringing good luck to his family. It is in the third line of the stanza that the relationship between the guest and the host is clarified, and is indicated that they are brother-in-laws. The discovery of this fact on the part of the reader gives the prevailing humour a new impetus. The fourth line of the stanza, "We have Manju and Trishala more," is quite humorous because the two girls are referred as if they are mere objects instead of being human beings. In the next two lines, the speaker reminds the host of the familial ties, which binds them together, and indirectly suggests that there is no escape from these responsibilities. Such a helpless condition of the host evokes good and gentle humour. In the seventh line of the stanza, the guest comes up with a new request and that is to find suitable matches for Manju and Trishala. The language and the tone of the poem makes the request look like 'demand', and it seems as if the visitor is commanding the host to fulfil his requirements. The visitor asks his brother-in-law to engage all his relatives in the hunt for suitable matches for both the girls. The repetition of the word 'relatives', for five times in quick succession, also helps in creating humour. The last three lines of the stanza display the influx of modern practices into the orthodox thinking of Indian people living in small towns or villages. The visitor in his urge to find a suitable match for the girls is ready to allow a meeting between the girl and the members of the family of the boy, but wants to arrange this meeting in such a way that no one comes to know of this. For maintaining the secrecy, he wants his brother-in-law to arrange for such a meeting, if any, at his own residence.

The depiction of such a situation is indeed humorous. The use of the phrase "Girl-seeing" heightens the humour, as it is a typical translation of the native term used for a meeting between the members of the family of a boy and the girl, before marriage.

In the first three lines of the next stanza, the visitor seeks the approval of his brother-in-law to send the two girls at his residence. To convince the host of his opinion, the visitor provides a pretext that the three sisters would enjoy each other's company for the period, thus adding to their happiness. In the next two lines, the visitor expresses his choice in regard to the matrimonial alliance of the two girls that he would prefer to marry them to boys not seeking any dowry. The last four lines of the stanza stand in complete contrast to the choice expressed by the visitor in relation to the marriage of the girls, and that of Ashok (probably his brother or son). Such a contrast in opinion is well reflected by the foregrounded sentence "he will be a full doctor soon" and the use of the word 'party' for such a family who seeks to get its girl married to Ashok. The poet cleverly foregrounds the seventh line of the stanza with the use of two stretched hyphens at both the ends of the sentence to convey that the line is not any ordinary one, but has more meanings to express. The visitor intentionally uses the word 'doctor' to label Ashok instead of a student of medicine, as it elevates his status, which could be better encashed by receiving more dowry. The situation is humorous as the speaker has clear intentions of receiving dowry for Ashok, whereas on the other hand, he is looking to get Manju and Trishala married without paying any dowry. The other notable point which generates humour is that the visitor leaves all such decisions at the discretion of his brother-in-law where his benefit is assured; whereas, in the case of fixing the marriage alliance of Ashok he does not grant him any decision making power.

In the first line of the seventh stanza, the visitor declares that he is meeting his brother-in-law after ages; whereas, in the very next line, he reveals that he has visited him only a few years before, when he had visited the place for the treatment of his old aunt. These two contrary statements produce humour. The first three lines also create humour in another sense as it discloses the fact that the speaker is a regular visitor to the host's house on some pretext or the other, and especially when there is any problematic situation, the host is made to suffer the pain each time. The next four lines of the stanza seem to be a digression from the main dialogue, but the poet very subtly associates it with the main topic of conversation. The guest informs his brother-in-law that Asha has to appear in a supplementary examination in Sociology, and for the purpose Shyamji has accompanied her to Jaipur.

In the next stanza the visitor resumes the main dialogue and informs his brother-in-law that Raju (Visitor's son) could not manage to pass in English this time, and has obtained a supplementary in the same. The use of the word 'unluckily' in the first line, and the third line "he never failed once in his life" to defend Raju from the allegations of not being a good student, evokes humour. The fourth and the fifth line is again a digression from the main dialogue and complete the information provided in the last few lines of the previous stanza. These digressions also serve as a cause to the creation of humour. In the next three lines, the speaker expresses his wish that the host would help Raju in passing the supplementary exams, and is thus back to his main business which is to extract maximum help from his brother-in-law. In the following four lines, the visitor praises the host and his wife for their kind heartedness, which is intended to receive a desired result. The cunning approach of the visitor throughout the poem results to humour. In the last two lines of the stanza, the visitor informs the reader that the host's wife is a perfect example of Indian housewife, as she believes in the rich traditional and cultural values such as *Atithi Devo Bhavah*. He further adds that their stay at the host's house may bring them some unexpected rewards. The expression of such a belief on the side of the guest is humorous and too ironical in the given context. It is quite evident since the beginning of the poem that the guest or the visitor has been only a surmounted pressure or burden on the host, and there are no signs of him bringing any good thing to the host or his family. Thus, the last line is undoubtedly, one of the finest examples of irony and humour in the given context.

The last stanza is the longest one and as expected it yields intense humour. The stanza begins with a narration of an incident that occurred long back, when the visitor and his brother-in-law (host) were students of class seven. One day, both of them received harsh treatment from their headmaster, and this was a turning point in the life of the visitor as he discontinued his studies thereafter, and as a result, he is a matric (class 10) fail working in a private firm. Whereas, on the other hand, the host continued with his studies and attained an MA degree, and has become a professor in the university. A reader observes that both the main characters in the poem were under similar circumstances in their childhood, but in the present time, they are two extremes as far as professional achievement is concerned. The contrast between the achievements of the two main characters evokes humour in the poem. The use of the term 'perfeshur' for 'professor' in the eighth line of the stanza adds to the humour as it justifies the speaker's academic achievements. The word 'perfeshur' has also a touch and tone of the native dialect of the speaker, which evokes humour. In the next three lines of the stanza, the speaker informs his brother-in-law that his son wants to pursue his higher studies (MA) from the same university where he is a professor, and therefore he seeks his assistance. The speaker requests his brother-in-law to help his son to get admission in his university. Yet another request on the part of the visitor adds to the humour. In the next line, the speaker informs that he is leaving by the evening train, which should had been a sort of a relief for the host otherwise, but it is not so;

as in the following line, the speaker reveals his intention of leaving back his son. It is here, that a reader comes to know that the visitor is also accompanied by his son, and this revelation at the end of the poem is indeed surprising. Adding to the surprise of the reader, the speaker at once declares that he is going to leave back his son at the host's house. The whole situation depicted in the stanza is humorous. We find a digression again in the midst of the main speech, when the visitor talks of his Seth's nature in the next two lines. Resuming the main speech from the sixteenth line of the stanza, the visitor asks his brother-in-law (host) to assure the admission of his son in his university. The tone of the visitor, slowly and gradually, changes to authoritative mode, and this evokes humour. The visitor is even ready to bribe any professor, if required, for getting his son admitted into the university. However, he knows pretty well that no one would look for money if his brother-in-law tries for his admission. In the last two lines of the stanza, the visitor assures that he would be sending the money through money order as he receives the news of his son's admission. Such an assurance on the part of the visitor leads to humour, as it is understood by the reader that the host will have to spend from his own pocket for all the related expenditures of the visitor's son, and the money would be refundable only on the subject of his getting admission in the university. The subtle depiction of the helpless condition of the host in the poem evokes humour.

While analysing the poem carefully, we observe that it is not only the context and content of the poem, which evokes humour; but the rhythm, tone, and structure of the poem contribute equally in the creation of humour. The unorganised stanza structure, i.e., different stanzas of different lengths; the conversation technique employed, i.e., only one speaker, and the listeners (probably two or three) have no active role to play; the use of poetic as well as prosodic techniques such as enjambment, digression, foregrounding, and others; typical use of punctuation marks to suggest more than what is expressed through the given lines; a touch of native dialect style etc., contribute remarkably in making the poem humorous.

Maha Nand Sharma does not use humour to such an extent as it is found in the poetry of I. K. Sharma. Most of the poems of Maha Nand Sharma do not create humour, and as a result, the poet looks to be very serious in his approach. We find humour only in some of his long narrative poems, especially at those places where he mocks the society or a class of people, in a light satiric vein. He requires large canvas to display humour unlike I.K. Sharma, who can create humour with subtle deftness even in small poems of eight or ten lines. In the poetry of Maha Nand Sharma, the humour is generally created more due to a situation or character than the use of the language.

Maha Nand Sharma, in his narrative poem 'The Professor-Critic and his Class of Poets' (p. 33) from *Gushing Streams*[10] creates humour in the depiction of the situation, and we may easily find an undercurrent of satire in the tone of the poem. Thus, the poem may be labelled as a humorous-satire on such critics and poets who acknowledge themselves as great literary figures, and in doing so they even go to the extent of criticising good literary works and real gems of literature. The first stanza of the poem displays a group of poets waiting for a visiting professor-critic under a banyan tree:

> Under a spreading banyan tree
> The poets sat on a mat.
> As wild as their fancies free
> Their class would hum and chat.

We find the setting of the poem itself to be humorous. The use of the words such as 'wild', 'fancies free', 'hum', and 'chat' in the third and the fourth line of the stanza indicates that the poets are not any ordinary persons, but distinct in their own class. The next stanza of the poem 'The Professor-Critic and his Class of Poets' builds upon this idea:

With beards o'ergrown and nails too long
And locks dishevelled, dry,
With hearts which throbbed with passion strong,
With hopes that never die,

The description of the poets in the stanza establishes them as a distinct class of people. The image of the poets depicted in the stanza identifies them as people who do not care at all about their physical appearance. The poets are depicted as people with overgrown beards, long nails, curly strands of hair, heart full of passion and immortal hopes. Such a depiction evokes humour.

The third stanza of the poem compares the poets with urchins, and it is further stated that they cannot stop writing poetry, as they feel uneasy when they are not productive:

Like urchins who would never shirk
Their work and feel at ease,
They too with their creative works
Their professor hoped to please.

The use of simile in the first line of the stanza to draw a comparison between poets and urchins evoke humour. We may also find irony in the last two lines of the stanza, as the poets write with an intention to please the critics and academicians, instead of pleasing the readers.

The next stanza describes the entry of Professor Ramsay Phagot on the scene:

The class was into silence tamed
When, quick as a striking thought
Or lightning in the heavens, came
Professor Ramsay Phagot.

The arrival of the Professor-Critic is marked by phrases such as 'quick as a striking thought' and 'lightning in the heavens' which indirectly indicate that the professor came out of nowhere, in other words, the actual roots of the professor are not known, and at the same time the professor seemed to be in a hurry. The use of such witty phrases in the stanza evokes humour.

The next stanza (p. 34) describes the appearance of the Professor-Critic:

> His neat-cut suit, his Oxford drawl,
> His well-pressed knotted tie,
> His bluish felt-hat awed them all—
> The poetry-ridden guys.

We find a total contrast in the appearance of the poets and the professor-critic, and this contrast evokes humour as it has the embedded idea that the person who studies (analyses or rather criticises) poetry, and thus depend on poets, is more fabulous than the persons creating poetry (poets). One notable feature of the stanza is the use of compound words such as 'neat-cut', 'well-pressed', 'felt-hat', and 'poetry-ridden', which indirectly reflects the compound or complex nature of the Professor-Critic. The contrast in the appearance and the use of one compound word in each line creates humour in the given stanza.

The glossy look of Professor Ramsay Phagot also grabs the attention of four great-recognised poets of their time, Shakespeare, Milton, Shelley, and Tagore:

> From far above in heaven looked
> At them the poets four—
> The wizard Shakespeare, Milton grouped
> With Shelley and Tagore.

The intellectual look of Phagot influences the four great poets to such an extent that they decide to descend down on earth to learn a few lessons of poetry from him:

> They thought "We should enjoy the fun
> Of poetry-learning there

On Earth where poets read with a Don
Who smartly takes a chair.

The idea of the four great poets, who devoted whole of their life to poetry, to learn poetry from a modern critic is trifle enough to create humour. The thought of coming down from Heaven to Earth, and that too, to learn few tips of poetry is humorous enough, but the humour gets intense when we discover that it is Shakespeare, Milton, Shelley, and Tagore, who are interested in joining this class for learning poetry. The use of the word 'Don' in the third line of the stanza is witty as it displays a multiple of meanings. The word 'Don' has an archaic use in the British context, where it means 'a teacher at a university, especially Oxford or Cambridge'; whereas, in the Indian context it means 'the leader of a group of criminals'. The juxtaposed meanings of the word 'Don' in the two different contexts create humour.

The succeeding stanza reveals clearly that the whole setting of the poem is Indian:

Since we'll now land in India, so
We should have Indian names.
Shakespeare will be called 'Sutto',
And Milton 'Singh' surnamed.

We may associate the information provided in the first two lines of the poem: "Under a spreading banyan tree / The poets sat on a mat" with this stanza we reach to a conclusion that the narrator is talking of the 'Gurukul' style of imparting knowledge. The revelation of this fact evokes humour, as Professor Ramsay Phagot is an alien to the whole setting. The four great poets decide to change their names in order to conceal their real identity, and the new names allocated to Shakespeare and Milton are 'Sutto' and 'Milton Singh' respectively. The change of names to 'Sutto' and 'Milton Singh', which sounds Indian, is humorous.

The next stanza (p. 35) narrates the enacting of the plan of the four poets:

"And 'Phuppur' will be Shelley's name
And 'Thakur' Tagore's be."
Ill dressed as poets below, they came
On Earth to have a spree.

The first two lines have a continuation of the humorous vein of the previous stanza as they disclose the fictitious names of Shelley and Tagore. The third line reminds us that the poets are ill dressed, and therefore the four poets descending from Heaven decide to adopt a similar ragged appearance.

The next stanza of the poem reveals that it is not only the four poets who have changed their names to conceal their real identities, but a similar trick had also been adopted by the Professor-Critic:

As poets four had changed their name
While coming down from Heaven,
The Don on Earth a similar game
Had played to make things even.

The stanza evokes humour as it depicts that the teacher, who is well dressed like an intellectual, is also befooling the students. It is not expected that a person looking to be such a great scholar would be involved in any sort of trickery, and the revelation of this fact evokes humour. Apart from infusing humour into the poem, the stanza also makes the reader anxious to find out the real story behind the Professor-Critic.

The succeeding stanza reveals the secret of the professor, who appears to be of western origin by this time:

Since "Ram Sahai Phogat," the name
Of Indian Don, was strange,

By him had earlier been the same
To 'Ramsay Phagot' changed.

The discovery of the real origin, i.e., Indian, of the Professor-Critic, and how he conceals his real identity by changing his name from "Ram Sahai Phogat" to "Ramsay Phagot" evokes humour. The use of the phrase 'Indian Don' adds to the humour taking into account the meaning of the word 'Don' in the Indian context. The stanza displays a perfect blending of humour and satire as it mocks at all such people who conceal their real identity to shoot to popularity. The narrator unleashes his contempt for all such Indians who change their names, religion, tradition, practices, and overall lifestyle to match with that of any foreign country.

The next stanza marks the beginning of Professor Ramsay's class:

The four new poets sat with the rest.
Professor asked their names.
"Now, Sutto, come," he said with zest.
And Shakespeare quickly came.

The use of a comma to separate all the three words of a command, uttered by the professor, imparts a humorous tone to the line, and the quick response that he gets from Shakespeare adds to the humour.

From the thirteenth stanza onwards, the narrator narrates the parameters on which a modern critic examines a poem, and indirectly suggests the reasons for the loss of the gloss of contemporary poetry. In the following stanzas we find a very rich and good blending of irony, satire, and humour. The thirteenth stanza (p. 36) presents a mockery on the Shakespearean style of writing poetry, but in real terms, it is a mockery on the ways or stipulations, which are taken into account by the contemporary critics while critically examining a piece of poetry:

'The most unkindest cut'—this line
Has double superlative.
'Unkindest cut' would have been fine.
How poor's your grammar, native!

Poetry is an art form, which overcomes the limitations of any language to fill the reader with joy and aesthetic pleasure, and therefore should not be constrained by any set of rules that are applicable to other forms of language or literary writing. The aesthetic appeal of any poem lies in its meaning, emotion, rhythm, and spontaneity, but not in the lexical items used or the structure of the sentences. In other words, poetry should not be judged on the rules of grammar. But in the stanza quoted above, the Professor-Critic passes a verdict on Shakespeare's poetry on the basis of the rules of grammar. Ramsay Phagot suggests Shakespeare not to use double superlatives in his poems, and this suggestion evokes humour. The stanza contains an undertone of satire, which ridicules such critics who criticize certain poems on a set of certain dogmatic rules or standards, instead of judging or analyzing a poem on its individual worth. Such critics have the tendency of deliberately finding faults with any poem on the basis of any certain parameter, which should not at all be considered while evaluating the merit of any poem.

The next stanza throws light on the dominating attitude of the professor:

As Sutto murmured, "Sir," the Don
With a birch-rod struck his joints:
By me a poet's worth is known
To the farthest decimal point.

When Sutto (Shakespeare) tries to intervene or raise a question to defend his poetic qualities, he is forced to silence. The harsh treatment, which Sutto receives at the hands of the Professor-Critic, justifies the use of the phrase 'Indian Don' for the professor. The next two lines of the stanza clearly reveal that the contemporary critics adopt mathematical standards while judging the merit of a poet. They place poets on a metrical scale and draw comparisons between them. This practice is not justified as each poet has his own unique style of writing poetry, and therefore, we should not compare two poets or measure the worth of any poet on any such parameter, which has mathematical standards. The last line of the stanza adds to the humour, as it is an assurance on the part of the professor-critic that he is competent to judge the poetic calibre of any poet flawlessly, which is not at all possible in real terms. Thus, we find that under the humorous tone and content of the stanza, there lies a satire on the modern critics who boast themselves to be very learned and unmistakably accurate in their findings.

In the next two stanzas, the narrator throws more light on the nature and achievements of the professor:

> I quote not; sift not; ne'er explain
> Nor furnish facts and figures,
> With sweeping statements I have slain
> The tallest men of letters.
>
> Minute are all my critical norms,
> Exact like Mathematics.
> On trivial themes I can perform
> My finest acrobatics.

Ramsay Phagot declares that he never gives a poem a serious thinking or examines it carefully before attempting an analysis of the same. He is neither in the habit of providing explanations for his findings nor does he ever refer to any other established source of information or set of rules. He just comments whatever is his first impression of a poem.

The last line of the fifteenth stanza displays that the Professor-Critic takes pride in saying that he has criticised or distorted the reputation of a number of established poets with his critical observations made on them. The last two lines of the fifteenth stanza display dramatic irony and at the same time evoke humour in the given context, as the Professor-Critic is not aware of the fact that he is yet again slaying the reputation of one of the best poets (Shakespeare) of all times, simultaneously with his speech. The reader, on the other hand, knows the real identity of Sutto, and this knowledge on the part of the reader establishes an incidental parallelism between what is said and what is happening, and that too, without the knowledge of the agent (Professor).

In the sixteenth stanza, the Professor-Critic talks astoundingly of the parameters on which he judges a poem, and tries to establish his competence. The critic himself discloses that he can create or project a mole into a mountain. The use of the words such as mathematics and acrobatics creates humour as they represent the critic's ability to make calculations and the same time give twists and turns to any simple thing respectively. Thus, we find a perfect blend of humour, irony, and satire in these stanzas.

In the next stanza (p. 37), the Professor-Critic moves with his analysis of Sutto's poetry:

> 'Tomorrow and tomorrow'—Ah !
> 'Tis boring repetition!
> Prosaic are all your lines. Pah !
> 'Tis poetry's perdition.'

It is known to everyone that repetition is used as a major poetic device by most of the poets, but the modern critic condemns its use as he finds it boring. He charges Sutto's poetry to be prosaic in nature, and in the last line indirectly declares that Sutto's (Shakespeare's) poetry is not worthy of study. The Professor-Critic's comment that poetry is being severely punished at the hands of Sutto (Shakespeare) provokes humour in a reader.

In the next stanza, Professor Ramsay commands Singh (Milton) to read his verse:

> "O shabby poet, bring your verse," –
> He called the poet, Singh,
> And Milton with a silent curse,
> Advanced with blushes tinged.

The way in which Phagot addresses Milton in the first line evokes humour. Although Milton knows that even his poetry is going to be severely criticised by the Professor-Critic, he does not dare to avoid or impeach the authority (Professor Ramsay).

The succeeding two stanzas depict the Professor's verdict on Milton's poetry:

> Absurd are all your lines, O Singh.
> If subject comes in one,
> Its object in the third you bring.
> Your work is all ill done.
>
> Some alienation there must be
> In modern poetry.
> But not the least of that I see
> In verses penned by thee.

Ramsay finds all Miltonic verses absurd, as the object does not closely follow its subject. Thus, we find that the Professor-Critic condemns verses written by Singh (Milton) for the very reason that brought popularity to it and is considered to be a hallmark of Miltonic verses. In the twentieth stanza, the Professor advocates the feature of alienation in modern poetry, and ridicules Singh for not considering such an important feature in his verses.

In the next stanza (p. 38), the Professor-Critic illustrates the technique of making verses modern in outlook and appeal to the group of poets:

'As curved as a boy's arc of piss',
'As tight as underwear'—
Such striking similes do not miss
Modernity's garb to wear.

The examples used for illustration evoke humour. Apart from being humorous, the stanza has an undertone of satire, which ridicules the use of words such as 'piss' and 'underwear' to provide a modern touch to the poem. The satire is directed towards such poets who call themselves modern and use derogatory words under the garb of modernity. In real terms, the use of such words, similes, metaphors, and contexts lead to nullify the aesthetic appeal of a poem.

The next stanza of the poem throws more light on the temperament and attitude of the Professor-Critic:

Then in a strident tone he called
The poet, Phuppur, straight.
No sooner had Professor bawled
He came with awkward gait.

The way in which Professor Phagot treats the group of poets is unjustifiable, and at the same time displays how great poets such as Shakespeare, Milton, and Shelley are also subdued by the modern critics. The treatment which the great poets are receiving at the hands of a modern snob surprises and amuses the readers, and thus evokes humour. The Professor calls 'Phuppur' in such an unpleasant, loud, and harsh tone that 'Phuppur' finds himself helpless and caught up in an uneasy situation. The stanza is a severe satire on all such critics and academicians who have such an arrogant attitude, or maintain a blatant relationship with poets.

In the next stanza, the Professor-Critic analyses the poetry of 'Phuppur' (Shelley):

'O World ! O Life ! O Time !'— Alas !

Your tears are false, O fool.
Romantic nonsense cannot pass.
It breaks the modern rule.

It is evident that the Professor-Critic does not approve of the verses written by 'Phuppur' (Shelley), who is representative of the romantic poets. Professor Phagot totally misjudges the tone and emotions lying in the poems of the romantic poets, and adjudges it as nonsense. The professor strictly abides by the modern parameters to judge even the romantic poetry, and therefore, he fails in making a correct analysis. But like any modern snob, the critic never accepts his failure and instead finds reasons to justify his findings or analysis.

In the succeeding stanza, the Professor-Critic instructs the poets to discard all necessary poetic qualities such as rules of rhetoric, rhythm, rhyme, poetic diction, and metre as they serve as fetters:

The rules of rhetoric, rhythm and rhyme,
The poetic diction, metres
Evolved so far since ancient times—
Discard them all as fetters.

Such a statement from an eminent looking scholar is ironical and at the same time humorous. The narrator indirectly states the reason for the sharp deterioration in the standards of poetry written in the contemporary age. The irony lies in the fact that first of all, the poets have stopped taking care of the important characteristic features of poetry to suit their convenience, and the next, even if some poets try their hands at writing good poetry, it is not well appreciated by the critics and academicians. Such an attitude on the part of the modern critics has marred the quality of poetry in the present age.

The next two stanzas (p. 39) depict the Professor-Critic's commentary on Thakur's (Tagore) poetry:

As Phuppur parted, Thakur came
By Don with promptness called,
In sober, mending tones the same
Was thus by Phagot bowled !

The English summer's warm; therefore,
Your summer warm must be.
With 'scorching, burning heat', O bore !
Your summer startles me.

Although the tone of the Professor-Critic is sober enough, the attitude remains the same, and he discards his poetry saying that the setting of his poems lies beyond the comprehension of the British people. Indirectly, the critic advises Thakur to write his poems in a foreign setting to receive proper acknowledgement and accreditation. Such a petty excuse or reason provided by the Professor-Critic for disapproving Thakur's poetry evokes humour. Here, the surprising element lies in the fact that the Professor-Critic has completely forgotten his roots, i.e., Indian origin, and therefore, he comments "Your summer startles me."

The twenty-seventh stanza is a perfect blend of humour, irony, and satire. In the stanza, the Professor-Critic asks Thakur to make Indians the subject of his poetry as they are a matter of talk and interest in the West:

'An Indian beggar begging alms'
'An Indian defecating
In fields !'—for poetry, Indians damned
Are subjects richly paying.

The surprising element in this stanza is that the same professor had advised Thakur to bring in foreign settings into his poetry, and now, he advises him to make Indians the subject of his poems. Such an advice displays the fluctuating nature of the Professor-Critic, and this evokes humour. We may also find an undercurrent of satire in the stanza as the narrator's hidden intention is to ridicule all such poets and authors, especially the diasporic writers, who use Indians as the subject of their writings not due to their deep association with them, but only to gain the attention of the western readers. These poets and writers intentionally highlight only the poor, sordid, gloomy, and pitiable state of India to satiate the western taste and receive applauds from them.

In the following stanza, the Professor-Critic marks out the deficiency of Thakur's (Tagore) poetry:

> Irreverence, alienation, sex—
> Modernity's features three,
> Their use your poetry badly lacks.
> This mars your poetry.

Professor Phagot remarks that Thakur's poetry is not up to the modern standards, because it lacks the three major elements or features of modernity, i.e., irreverence, alienation, and sex. Thus, according to Professor Phagot, one should make use of irreverence, alienation, and sex to elevate the standard or quality of their poetry, and to satiate the modern taste.

The next stanza (p. 40) displays rich blending of humour, sarcasm, and satire:

> 'Where knowledge is free'—what nonsense this
> Each college charges fee.
> O Thakur, stand not. Go and piss.
> The poetry's not for thee.

The remarks made by the Professor-Critic evokes humour although it's sarcastic in intend. A contemporary Professor-Critic asking a Nobel laureate to stop writing poetry as he has found him to be unfit for the same displays a humorous situation. The tone of the stanza and the use of the phrase 'Go and piss' results to sarcasm in the stanza. From the reader's point of view, the stanza displays only humour and sarcasm; whereas, if the narrator's point of view is taken into account, the lines seem to be a satire on all such contemporary scholars, critics, and academicians, who are not sensible enough to understand the true worth and quality of poetry, but does not desist from making derogatory statements on any great poet on the basis of their shallow understanding.

In the next stanza, the narrator narrates the helplessness of the four great poets, which force them to disappear from the scene:

> Professor Ramsay continued.
> The strangers disappeared.
> From Heaven they his teaching viewed
> And heartily laughed and jeered !

The four poets return to Heaven and heartily laugh at the teachings of the Professor-Critic. This situation evokes humour.

The following stanza is humorous enough to evoke boisterous laughter:

> A fine laughing stock is this,
> To foreign fads a slave.
> How pleasant it will be to piss
> Upon this shallow knave !

By this time the four poets have well understood that Professor Ramsay Phagot has no knowledge of poetry, or any poetic sense at all, and he only imitated certain modern and western views. They finally decide to piss over Phagot and equal scores with him for the harsh treatment that they had received at his hands. Such an idea evokes boisterous laughter.

The final stanza attains the peak of humour as it has the potential to burst any person with laughter:

> From Heaven their streaming arcs of piss
> Upon the Professor fell.

He upward looked. "What bird is this?"
He asked. But none could tell.

The situation depicted in the stanza may lead even any serious person to laughter. The four poets piss upon Professor Phagot from Heaven, and Phagot thinks that it is some sort of a bird that has discharged its excreta over him. The Professor enquires about the bird from his class of poets, but none could recognise the bird. In the stanza, the bird is a symbol used to represent true poetry, which is in turn represented by the four poets. Apart from evoking humour, the final stanza is also a satire on all such poets who change their style of poetry to suit the modern trend, thus abiding by the guidelines of a modern critic. By adopting such a course of poetry, the poets loose the original track of poetry and are misled to such an extent that they are even not able to recognise or identify true poetry.

When we read the whole narrative poem at a stretch, we find that Maha Nand Sharma maintains a uniform rhyme scheme of 'abab,' which provides smoothness to the rhythm and tone of the poem. The smooth rhythm and tone helps to the cause of evoking humour throughout the poem, as it keeps the reader into its tight hold or prevent him from any sort of digression, thus helping in the building up of humour. We may also note that the key lexical items, which result in the evolution of humour, are 'stressed' throughout the poem. The stress on these key words help in the generation of humour, as it paves the path for a better and quick comprehension on the part of the reader. Another notable feature of the poem is the development and depiction of the plot in his narratives. The plot is depicted with such minute details that a reader feels directly associated, and personally experiences the narrated events, as a result, the communication becoming more effective.

The poem 'If' or 'A Politician's Precepts to his Son' from *Scattered Leaves*[11] is a parody of Rudyard Kipling's famous poem "If". The fact cannot be ignored that parody is used as an effective tool to evoke satire, sarcasm, and humour. Although the poem does not display any humorous element superficially, it is successful in evoking a humorous reaction in the reader. The poem could be better understood on the principles of 'Rasa Siddhanta.' The humorous reaction received from one is due to the generation of 'hasya rasa' in him or her. An attempt has been made here to explain that how the 'hasya rasa' emerges in a reader? A reader always develops a context while reading any literary piece to understand it better. The subject around which the poem is built always has an influence over the readers, as they have certain ideas associated with the subject. Whenever a reader reads anything, he simultaneously associates it with his past experiences or knowledge to gain a better understanding of the same, and in the process, if he finds the idea expressed to be in juxtaposition or contrast with his past experiences or knowledge, he is surprised and amused, thus paving the path for the evolution of humour. The image of politicians is one of the leading concerns of most of the contemporary poets, and as soon as a reader gets to know that there is a talk of contemporary politicians in the given piece, he prepares himself for some humorous or satirical remarks. Such a preparation or an expectation on the part of the reader makes the job of the poet easier. The poet may either directly introduce the humorous content or present it in an indirect way as Maha Nand Sharma does here. When the humour is directly introduced, it may be easily traced with the help of the lexical items and ideas conveyed through them; but when a poet chooses the other way, the evolution of humour depends on the knowledge of the reader that he has in regard to the topic or subject of discussion. The things discussed or revealed in a poem either match a reader's experience or are in contradiction with his ideas and knowledge. Anyhow, in both the cases 'humour' may be easily generated. A common and general expectation of any person from a political leader is that the leader would lead him to welfare and progress, but one is astonished to notice the real faces and malicious intentions of the political leaders. When a poet talks of this real image of contemporary politicians in a satiric or sarcastic tone, it serves as a vent for the reader to unleash his anger, surprise, and anxiety in the form of laughter, and thus humour comes to play its role.

The other factor that makes the poem humorous is parody. Maha Nand Sharma develops the whole poem in the style of Rudyard Kipling's 'If,' but the objective and contents of his poem is in complete contradiction with the original one. Kipling's 'If' is a motivational or inspirational poem, which boosts the confidence of any reader; whereas, Sharma's 'If' is a sarcastic poem, which teaches or informs one of all the negative characteristics or qualities of a politician in such a way that they appear to be the positive qualities which a politician must possess. When we read Sharma's poem having read the Kipling's, we are bound to laugh and enjoy the disparity:

> If you can loudly preach but practice not,
> And slyly pull the strings from far behind;
> If you can change your stand with not a jot
> Of pain, in subtle plausible words refined;
> If you can grease the palm to please the flocks
> Of those with whom the way to wealth is lined;
> If you can use the toughs, for money bought,
> For blotting out your questioning rivals blind;
> ....
> ....
> If you can bear to be, by *chappals,* hit
> And say a Gandhian victory you have won;
> If you can be a crook, a thief, a hermit,
> A person chaste, a lecher—all in one;
> If you can get released, notorious culprits
> And count thick wads of notes when the day is done;
> Yours is the Earth and everything that's in it
> And—which is more—you'll be a man, my son.

The poem is written in the same structure as that of the Kipling's, i.e., four stanzas of eight lines each. The only apparent difference, which a reader can make between the two poems, is in the use of punctuation marks. The long stanzas of the poem helps in providing a bigger canvas, which makes it easier to increase the intensity of humour, and the humour goes on piling with each successive line. A reader gets a short respite from humour only at the end of a stanza, and the succeeding stanza again picks up the humour from the same level. The poem is written in a conversational tone, where a politician is passing his words of wisdom and experience to his son. One notable feature of the first three stanzas is that they begin with a quotation mark but does not end with the same. This indicates that the preaching continues and does not come to an end. Again, the next stanza starts with a fresh quotation mark, displaying that the politicians are in a habit of leaving the previous work unaccomplished, and meanwhile starting a new project without predicting its accomplishment. This depiction highlights one of the characteristic traits of the contemporary politicians, and evokes humour. Another notable feature of the poem is the use of only one 'period' (full stop), and that too at the end of the poem, suggesting that despite of all the disturbances or temporary stoppages (marked by commas and semi-colons), a politicians heads his way to a conclusion with the attainment of his personal motifs.

We find the poem to be a perfect example of the blending of 'humour' and 'sarcasm'. By analyzing the poem, we easily understand that how 'sarcasm' yields to 'humour'. The first stanza of the poem straightaway introduces a reader to the precepts or preaching of a politician to his son. The first line unveils one of the characteristic features of a politician, which suggests that a politician is always a 'hypocrite'. The second line displays the cunning attitude of a politician, as he uses his agents to deceive the innocent people. The third line uncovers the 'unreliable' nature of the contemporary politicians.

The next line throws enough light on the 'deceptive speech' of any politician. The next two lines depict the 'meanness' of any politician, as he is ever ready to please the wealthy and rich people for his personal interests. The last two lines of the stanza display the 'anti-social and criminal' aspect of a politician, as he uses certain anti-social elements to suppress the voices raised against him. By the end of the stanza, a reader is thoroughly informed that a politician is a hypocrite, deceptive, unreliable, mean, and an anti-social element. The image of a politician depicted in the stanza is in utter contrast to the image of an ideal politician. The revelation of this contrast between 'what is expected' and 'what is discovered' surprises a reader, and thus evokes humour in the poem.

The second stanza of the poem reveals some more characteristic information about a politician. A politician not only deceives innocent people, but also the seniors and masters of his political party. He butters his immediate seniors for gaining power or ascendance, and then betrays them, whenever he finds an opportunity, by disclosing their secrets to the big masters of the political party to gain more power and higher position. The poem thus suggests that a politician is not faithful to anyone, and is a perfect embodiment of 'deceptiveness' and 'ingratitude'. In a way, the stanza provides enough details to convince a reader that a politician does not bias between a common person and even his masters, as he maintains the same double standards for all of them, and thus treats them alike. One is convinced to accept the opinions expressed by the poet, as he makes a politician his mouthpiece, and the whole poem is developed in the form of a precept that the politician professes to his son. The technique of communication adopted in the poem reflects the poet's wit, and distinguishes him as a master in the poetic art.

In the third stanza, the poet hints at the public image of a politician, and displays that how a politician misuses his good image to deceive common people. A politician appears to be a 'Messiah' to the common folks, but in reality he is an undertaker of their welfare and progress; he gains the trust and confidence of common people to reward them with penury and pain. The sixth and the seventh line suggest that a politician can never be loyal to anyone, and he betrays both the classes of people, i.e., rich and poor. He gets closer to the rich for gaining monetary contributions; whereas, he develops close ties with the poor to gain their votes. The last two lines highlight the corrupt attitude of the contemporary politicians further. One notable feature of the stanza is the use of the word 'Messiah' for the corrupt politicians, as it is not only satirical but also evokes humour.

The last stanza of the poem very briefly reinstates all the characteristic qualities, which any contemporary politician must possess. The first two lines suggest that a contemporary politician has no regard for his self-respect as well, and he can stake his self-respect for gaining materialistic ends. The next four lines recapitulate all the characteristics of a politician in a humorous tone, thus adding to the humour. Maha Nand Sharma retains the last two lines of the Kipling's poem, as it is, to end his poem as well. These lines take humour to its new height as the politician in the poem preaches all negative, unmanly, and inhuman traits to his son throughout the poem; and finally, assure him that if he is able to inculcate all those virtues, which are vices in real terms, he would become a great man. Such an assurance from a father-politician is quite amusing, and thus evokes humour. One notable feature in the last line of the poem is that the poet uses a small alphabet 'm' in 'man'; whereas, the original poem (Kipling's "If") has it as 'Man.' This minute observation on the part of the reader evokes humour and at the same time reflects the satiric intend of Sharma.

The above study displays and illustrates that Maha Nand Sharma and I. K. Sharma use humour as a very effective tool for poetic communication, and it also establishes that humour is the best possible tool to comment on the contemporary society.

References

1. Anonymous. http://www.angelfire.com/ne/cre8vityunltd/humor.html
2. http://www.iep.utm.edu/h/humor.htm
3. http://psychcentral.com/news/2008/06/30/the-evolution-of humor/2523.html
4. http://www.iep.utm.edu/h/humor.htm
5. Kant, Immanuel. *Critique of Judgment.* J. H. Bernard, Trans. New York: Hafner. 1951. p.54.
6. http://psychcentral.com/news/2008/06/30/the-evolution-of- humor/2523.html
7. Chaudhury, Pravas Jivan. "The Theory of Rasa", *The Journal of Aesthetics and Art Criticism.* Vol.24, No.1, Autumn 1965. pp 145-149.
8. Sharma, I.K. *My Lady, Broom and Other Poems.* Jaipur: Sand-Pra Publications, 2004. p. 27.
9. ——. *The Shifting Sand-Dunes.* Jaipur: Jaipur Publishing House, 1976. pp. 31-34.
10. Sharma, Maha Nand. *Gushing Streams.* Meerut: Mrs. Krishna Sharma, 1996. p. 33.
11. ——. *Scattered Leaves.* Meerut: Ashutosh Prakashan, 1991. p. 15-16.

14

'Sarcasm' as a Tool of Poetic Communication: A Comparative Study of Maha Nand Sharma and I. K. Sharma

Ram Kulesh Thakur and *R. K. Singh*

On the basis of the Jakobson's model of communication, a poem is a communicative act. In constructing the meaning of a text, one needs to take into account all the categories participating in the communication such as sender (poet or author), receiver (reader or audience), contact, message, code, and context. A poet's use of language is much different from that of any other writer. A poet uses various tools, rhetorical devices, and pragmatic structures to build his unique literary style. The paper discusses and establishes 'sarcasm' as one of the prominent tools employed in poetic communication. It studies the poetry of Maha Nand Sharma and I. K. Sharma to trace the evolution of sarcasm from the rhetorical use of language in a certain context.

'Sarcasm' stems from the Greek word 'sarkazein', which means 'to tear the flesh, to bite.'[1] It involves the use of cutting, contemptuous, biting, derisive, bitter, mordant, or sardonic remarks, delivered often in a hostile manner. The manner of delivery is often very important; for the tone must be such that one recognises that someone is attacking someone else and making a sarcastic remark.[2] It evolves out of a witty language that is used to convey insults or scorn. Sarcasm is also charged to be a low form of humour as its intent is generally to get laughs at someone else's expense. The pointed humour may not be funny to the victim but it's funny to those who understand the barb as it feeds their intellectual egos.[3] This is because sarcasm is a form of humour that is known to require the highest functions of our brains. Areas of the brain that decipher sarcasm and irony also process language, recognise emotions, and help understand social cues.[4] Therefore, it may be stated that sarcasm is related to one's ability to understand other people's mental state and thus it is not just a linguistic form but is also associated with social recognition.[5] It is part of pragmatic communication; the knowledge of the language code alone cannot help in interpretation of the poem. For correct and proper understanding of the literary text, especially poetry, one needs to have an adequate understanding of the literary style of the poet. Most of the poems where sarcasm is used as a vehicle of poetic communication takes into account the culture, tradition, and the archetypal views of the morals rooted in the domestic context. Therefore, it becomes necessary that the reader is well exposed to the culture and tradition of the place to which the poet belongs, for a correct and appropriate interpretation of the message encoding the poems. If readers are unaware of the domestic archetypal practices, they may not understand the satire or sarcasm that is subtly in operation. In this context, it is also necessary to distinguish sarcasm from the other very closely associated concepts such as parody and satire as all three poke fun at people. The difference among the three concepts is a subtle one and lies mainly in the motivation behind their use.

This motivation or intent is clearly reflected by the pragmatic use of the language, i.e., selection of words and their arrangement to form a sentence in a context. The tone of the sentence also plays a very vital role in adjudging its characteristic or nature whether it is ironic, satiric, sarcastic, or humorous. The intent behind parody is just to have fun— to make people laugh. It lacks any intent to do harm; whereas, satire intents to make fun of people's follies and foibles with a hope of producing a change in their behaviour. Satire's purpose is to produce better people—not simply to crack a joke or hurt. The satirist trusts in the basic worth of his target and believes that with a little prodding that target can become a better person.[6] On the other hand, sarcasm's intent is to wound its target. Sarcasm tears apart with no intention of putting back together; whereas, satire cuts but does so carefully so that the parts may be reassembled after the corrections have been made. Satire is basically a mode of writing that exposes the failings of individuals, institutions, or societies to ridicule or scorn. It is often an incidental element in literary works that may not be wholly satirical, especially in comedy. There may be a variation in tone in the case of a satire; whereas, the tone is always high and uniform in the case of sarcasm. Thus, it may be stated that it is the tone that distinguishes sarcasm.

Maha Nand Sharma's usage of language is stunning in some of his poems as he uses very strong words to create beautiful mental images for the reader about everyday life. An analysis of the poem entitled 'A Tale of Freedom's Tears' from *Scattered Leaves*[7] presents the distinct and unique way in which the poet creates sarcasm in his poems. The poem is a satire on the different forms of government and the prevailing corruption all over. The poem indirectly questions the need of a system in which a few people rule or govern the remaining lot. The poem develops a sarcastic tone in stanza 39, and thereafter we find a rich and fine blending of wit, humour, satire, and sarcasm. In some of the stanzas, the sarcasm is interspersed with satire and it is only the tone of the poem that differentiates the both:

> They talked of legislators dressed
> In handloom dhoties, shirts so white
> That in its whiteness, purity too
> Could hardly match a dress so white.
>
> (Stanza 39)

In the last three lines, we find a very rich blending of wit, humour, and sarcasm. The legislators project themselves in such a way that they are the idols of honesty and perfection. The noteworthy point in the stanza is that 'purity' is an abstract concept that requires no definition. Purity itself means that it is taintless, complete, and perfect; the whiteness of purity is therefore unquestionable. However in the stanza, the poet compares the whiteness of a legislator's shirt with the whiteness of purity itself, and this evokes humour. The sarcasm in the stanza is created when the poet claims that the whiteness of a legislator's shirt dazzles purity too. The poet mocks the attitude of the politicians who put on a garb of purity to cheat their followers. The whiteness of their shirt is in absolute contrast to their real nature, which is deceitful, selfish, and cunning. The poet suggests that a legislator wears such a white shirt with a malicious intention and that is to hide the dark aspects of his personality. The tone of the lines makes it easy for the reader to trace that it is sarcasm at play, as we find in the next stanza:

> Of honest bosses they would talk
> Who touched not pelf beyond their due,
> Who talked of conscience day and night
> And said, they never spoke but true.
>
> (Stanza 40)

The poet induces a subtle sarcasm along with humour in the second line where he talks of the 'honest bosses' who kept themselves away from corruption. In the stanza, the word 'honest' is used in a different context and sense, other than what the reader expects. Here, the word honest is used in a context to show that the bosses are fair and dependable where the distribution of money earned through corrupt means is concerned. The bosses are only interested in collecting their share or due of the black money. It is the use of the word 'honest' and the phrase 'touched not pelf beyond their due' that creates sarcasm in the stanza. The irony and tone of the line is also of great help in evoking sarcasm in the above mentioned stanza. Here, the poet's apparent praises conceal another, scornful meaning. Thus, we find that Maha Nand Sharma does not always express sarcasm blatantly and has the ability to convey it in an exaggerated intonation of tone, which over-accentuates and draws attention to what is being mocked. In the succeeding stanza 41:

> They talked about professors great,
> Inventing numerous 'ologies'
> To which they raised e'en topics small,
> Exhausting all morphologies.

The poet creates sarcasm by suggesting that the professors are over-competent to such an extent that they can even raise a small topic to such a height that it becomes a subject of study and research, and in the process they make use of all the existing morphologies. It is the punch of the last line, "Exhausting all morphologies," that provides a sarcastic colour to the ironical statements made in the preceding lines of the stanza. The sarcasm is created in the stanza, taking into consideration the deplorable condition of research in most of the Indian Universities. The professors who are tagged as 'great' do not take adequate interest in research and just while away their time dealing with petty topics of no academic worth. These professors project themselves as great intellectuals by using big and high sounding words in their usual talks and discussions. It is with the use of their subtle language that they make small things appear worthy of attention and distinctive study.

Again, in the next two stanzas of the poem, we find sarcasm:

> But as I strolled among the dons,
> 'Midst judges, bosses, M.L.A.'s,
> And senators great and M.P.'s stern,
> Their stinking guiles my conscience flayed.
>
> For each pursued the bubbles bright
> Of wealth, of lust, of pow'r unreined,
> E'en lost for them his conscience pure
> And, like chamelions, colours changed.

In the last line of stanza no.42, the poet uses the phrase 'stinking guiles' as a characteristic trait of few reputed persons such as professors, bosses, MLAs, senators, and MPs, which is sarcastic. The use of the word 'stinking' as a modifier to the term 'guiles' adds to the bitterness of the sarcasm. The next stanza shows an immaculate blending of wit and sarcasm. The first two lines are rich in wit whereas the last two lines add sarcasm. Eminent people such as MLAs, MPs, judges, senators, and others are compared with chameleons, and it is at this juncture that sarcasm is infused by the poet with the aid of a simile. Another noteworthy feature in these two lines is the repetition of the consonant sound 'k', which inducts harshness to the tone of the poem and thus aids the purpose of sarcasm.

From stanzas 44 to 54 of this long narrative poem, we observe only wit, humour, irony, and satire playing their roles one after the other; no instance of sarcasm is found. However, once again in stanza 55:

> In seminars, if one questioned Heads,
> Their toughs would shout one down at once.

Such service won them high degrees
With knowledge less than that of a dunce.

The poet creates sarcasm in the final line of the stanza where he states that even such people are awarded high academic degrees, whose knowledge is less than that of a dunce. The use of the word 'dunce' creates sarcasm in the stanza.

In stanza 58, we again find interspersion of satire and sarcasm:

In institutions widely known
For high research in science and arts,
Frustrated juniors hanged themselves-
Their findings grabbed by seniors smart.

In the last line of the stanza, the use of the phrase 'seniors smart' for such guides and supervisors who look for an opportunity to steal their juniors' findings is sarcastic. The use of the word 'smart' creates sarcasm, as the word is not used in a normal sense. The poet creates a pun over the word 'smart'. The word has no association with its actual literal meaning but suggests 'cunningness' in the stanza. The poet mocks at the attitude of such seniors who does not hesitate to make use of their juniors' findings for their personal motifs; debarring the junior from the fruit of his hard work.

Sarcasm is again very strongly displayed in the two consecutive stanzas 60 and 61:

The lion's share Professor had;
The toothless tigers, Readers, roamed.
Bereft of e'en the least of pow'r,
Like donkeys loaded, lecturers groaned.

Like dogs for crumbs of buttered bread,
They fought for tempting sinecures,
For them would sell their conscience cheap
By making wily overtures.

In the above stanzas, sarcasm is clearly reflected as the faculties of a university are compared with wild animals; a professor is said to be a lion in respect of his power; a reader is designated equivalent to a tiger, which suggests that even readers are ferocious by nature, but find themselves helpless as they do not have enough power to make things go in accordance to their respective choices. The poet depicts the actual scenario of Indian Universities where a professor is in the commanding position and always dominates the faculties who are lower to him. The lecturers are compared with donkeys in respect to the tremendous work load. The poet suggests that it is the lecturers who share the maximum burden of teaching and their position is no better than a donkey. The first line of the next stanza adds bitterness to the flowing sarcasm as all the faculties of the university are together compared with dogs fighting for crumbs of bread. The sarcasm in the stanza does not only gain strength from the pragmatics of the sentence but also from the realisation of the actual social scenario as depicted by the poet. The fact can never be ignored that a poet is a product of his environment and time. When we investigate into the personal life of the poet, we discover that Maha Nand Sharma has himself been a faculty at Meerut University for a long time. Thus, we are assured that whatever is being depicted is undoubtedly true and an outcome of the poet's personal experiences. This revelation makes the poem more sarcastic. The poet creates sarcasm in a very different manner in the 69th stanza of the poem:

> In parliaments the paper-weights
> Were flying, whizzing; mikes were hurled;
> The clothes were torn to shreds; to fight
> The M.P.'s their moustaches twirled.

In this stanza, the creation of sarcasm is very subtle as it is done with the help of a cultural context. The first three lines of the stanza narrate the episode where the so called leaders (politicians) of the country are engaged in a fight and that too, inside the parliament. The last line, "The M.P.'s their moustaches twirled" creates sarcasm in the poem, as twirling of moustaches has a meaning of taking pride in one's deeds and one twirls his moustaches only when one is proud of his action, in the cultural context. Thus, the stanza suggests that the politicians instead of being ashamed over their violent and shameful act are rather proud of it. Any reader who has the knowledge of Indian tradition and culture would never miss the subtle sarcasm in the stanza.

After a thorough analysis of one of the long narrative poems of Maha Nand Sharma, a few poems of I.K. Sharma are selected to trace sarcasm and the role played by it in the act of poetic communication. The first poem is 'The Pink City' from the collection *The Shifting Sand Dunes*, 1976: [8]

> This is a very unfortunate city.
> Conceived as a red rose
> in the hot sands
> in the distant dreams of a royal master
> counted, calculated, master-planned
> with precision of a modern mind
> has patterned into a handsome hell,
> ....
> ....
> every moment, for nose and eyes :
> ecology and economics merged into one.
> A vile reward for the red rose
> that has no thorns !

In the first stanza of the poem, the poet uses the phrase 'handsome hell' for the city of Jaipur, which is also known as the Pink City. The use of the phrase 'handsome hell' is witty and sarcastic at the same time. The permutation between the words 'handsome' and 'hell' does not go smooth as they combine to give an ambiguous meaning. The word 'handsome' is used as a modifier to highlight the characteristic of 'hell', which is quite ironical. The phrase also indicates a deep association between the persona of the poem and the city. Although, the persona is hurt to see the existing condition of the city, he is unable to dissociate himself from the good memories of the city, which he had experienced; the impact resulting in the use of the word 'handsome'. However, the phrase as a whole is undoubtedly sarcastic. We observe that in the third line of the second stanza, the poet eradicates the difference between a man and a pig to bring them together on the same plane with equal status. Both, a man (human) and a pig (animal), are said to be living in gutter and such a statement is undoubtedly sarcastic. Again, in the ninth and the tenth line of the same stanza, the poet's statement, "Man's mind chained by pigs and tied to them", is sarcastic. This statement adds bitterness to the sarcasm prevailing in the stanza as it suggests that it is not only the living conditions but also the thinking, which brings human being closer to pigs. Then again, in the seventh, eighth, and ninth line of the third stanza, the poet inducts sarcasm in a very subtle manner. Although, the lines do not exhibit any sarcasm at the pragmatic level of the sentence, the sarcasm is hidden in the view expressed. The poet wants to state that, because the people are paying tax to the government, they get an unsigned license to pollute the environment and disturb the ecological balance.

In the poem 'The Quest for Mother' from the collection *The Shifting Sand-Dunes*, we observe that sarcasm is created in the last few lines of the poem. The first two stanzas of the poem are rich in wit, irony, and satire. It is in the third stanza that the poet injects sarcasm:

> In the birth before, the breast had no rest,
> the child's nest, the lover's rest,
> and endlessly flowed the milk
> of love and life,

of kindness and humanity.
Now, a soother for subtle barbarians,
a dead, dry, dehumanised
symbol of self-pity and publicity,
geometrically draped, arithmetically calculated,
and socialised in capitalist waters.

It is observed that in the last five lines of the poem, the poet uses derisive statements for a contemporary woman's breast. The use of the words and phrases such as, 'dead'; 'dry'; 'dehumanized'; 'publicity'; 'geometrically draped'; 'arithmetically calculated'; and 'socialised in capitalist waters', for a contemporary woman's breast creates sarcasm in the poem. With the help of the sarcasm in the last few lines of the poem, the poet strongly ridicules the changing attitude of contemporary women towards child rearing. The poet expresses contempt towards such woman who are more worried over maintaining their physical appearance to make themselves presentable, rather than inheriting the elegance of womanhood.

In the poem 'Happy Home' from the same collection, we again find the poet creating sarcasm in the last few line. From the beginning of the poem we find interplay of wit and humour, but it is in the last three lines that the poet creates sarcasm:

...greets the day-worn man
not like an air-hostess
with a pre-fabricated smile.

In these lines, the poet is depicting a woman greeting her husband and the greeting is unlike that of an air-hostess. It is the phrase 'pre-fabricated smile' that creates sarcasm in the lines. Here, the poet suggests that the warm response that any passenger gets from an air-hostess is merely a part of her profession and is a readymade stuff, without any personal regard attached to it.

After a detailed analysis of a few poems of both the

poets, we can easily reach to a conclusion that both the poets rely upon sarcasm as a tool to communicate their views, ideas, and personal opinions through the medium of poetry. We also observe that among both the poets, Maha Nand Sharma relies heavily on sarcasm as a tool to communicate. I.K. Sharma uses sarcasm only as a catalyst to provoke the thoughts of his readers and give a jerk to shed off the monotony of the tone of any poem.

The sort of language employed by both the poets to create sarcasm is entirely different from each other. Maha Nand Sharma generally uses informal language such as, 'match a dress so white'; 'touched not pelf beyond their due'; 'never spoke but true'; 'strolled among'; 'stinking guiles'; 'like chameleons, colours changed'; 'shout one down'; 'that of a dunce'; 'grabbed by seniors smart'; 'lion's share professor had'; 'toothless tigers, Readers roamed'; 'like donkeys loaded, lecturers groaned'; 'dogs for crumbs'; 'tempting sinecures'; 'wily overtures'; 'moustaches twirled'; and many others, to produce sarcasm in his poems. On the other hand, I.K. Sharma uses formal language such as, 'handsome hell'; 'Both cross'; 'chained by pigs and tied to them'; 'dead'; 'dry'; 'dehumanized'; 'geometrically draped'; 'arithmetically calculated'; 'socialised in capitalist waters'; 'pre-fabricated'; and similar expressions to generate sarcasm in his poems. The tone of the language employed by Maha Nand Sharma is more biting and harsh than the other poet. I.K. Sharma generally blends humour with sarcasm, and more often a reader finds the tone of his poems humourous rather than biting.

When a number of other poems of Maha Nand Sharma are studied and analysed, pragmatically and socio-linguistically, we find that he often shifts his mode from satire to sarcasm and back to satire. He also creates an immaculate blend of wit, irony, humour, satire, and sarcasm in most of his long narrative poems and handles all of them remarkably well. On the other hand, I.K. Sharma uses wit, irony, humour, satire, and sarcasm distinctively in all his poems. It is hard to find any poem from his collections in which he changes his tool from one to the other and turn back to the earlier one. He uses more of wit, humour, irony, and satire to express himself rather than sarcasm.

Maha Nand Sharma creates sarcasm in his poems by placing two contrasting or juxtaposing things together as well as by using certain archetypal social and cultural morals. On the other hand, I.K. Sharma uses only his language in a subtle manner to create sarcasm. He blends humour and sarcasm inextricably well, whereas Maha Nand Sharma is a master in the blending of satire and sarcasm.

The way in which both the poets use sarcasm for poetic communication, clearly projects that Maha Nand Sharma is more displeased and discontented with the society. The use of sarcasm also reflects that the poet's hope of seeing a resurrection in the society is dying slowly and gradually. On the other hand, I.K. Sharma believes in the worth of the society and is still hopeful, as well as confident that the evils of the society would not last longer.

References

1. http://en.wikipedia.org/wiki/Sarcasm
2. Berger, Arthur Asa. *An Anatomy of Humor.* New Jersey: Transaction Publishers, 1991. p.49.
3. http://blogpond.com.au/2008/03/03/the-getting-of-sarcasm/
4. *Ibid.*
5. Byrnes, Dan. "Irony in US Literature and Life, contemporary." http://www.danbyrnes.com.au/irony.htm
6. Kittle, Jim R. "Satire: Tool of the Surgeon." http://my.opera.com/lounge/forums/topic.dml?id=69951
7. Sharma, Maha Nand. *Scattered Leaves.* Meerut: Ashutosh Prakashan, 1991.
8. Sharma, I.K. *The Shifting Sand Dunes.* Jaipur: Jaipur Publishing House, 1976.

Index